LAW
ENFORCEMENT
AGENCIES

DRUG
ENFORCEMENT
ADMINISTRATION

LAW ENFORCEMENT AGENCIES

Bomb Squad

Border Patrol

Crime Lab

Drug Enforcement Administration

Federal Bureau of Investigation

Interpol

Los Angeles Police Department

New York Police Department

The Secret Service

SWAT Teams

The Texas Rangers

U.S. Marshals

LAW
ENFORCEMENT
A G E N C I E S

DRUG
ENFORCEMENT
ADMINISTRATION

Michael Newton

CHELSEA HOUSE
An Infobase Learning Company

DRUG ENFORCEMENT ADMINISTRATION

Chelsea House
An imprint of Infobase Learning
132 West 31st Street
New York NY 10001

Library of Congress Cataloging-in-Publication Data

Newton, Michael, 1951–
Drug Enforcement Administration / Michael Newton.
p. cm. — (Law enforcement agencies)
Includes bibliographical references and index.
ISBN-13: 978-1-60413-641-8 (alk. paper)
ISBN-10: 1-60413-641-3 (alk. paper)
1. United States. Drug Enforcement Administration—Juvenile literature.
2. Drug control—United States—Juvenile literature. I. Title.
HV5825.N497 2011   363.25'9770973—dc22
2010036940

Chelsea House books are available at special discounts when purchased in bulk quantities for businesses, associations, institutions, or sales promotions. Please call our Special Sales Department in New York at (212) 967-8800 or (800) 322-8755.

You can find Chelsea House on the World Wide Web at
http://www.infobasepublishing.com

Text design and composition by Erika K. Arroyo
Cover design by Keith Trego
Cover printed by Bang Printing, Brainerd, Minn.
Book printed and bound by Bang Printing, Brainerd, Minn.
Date printed: February 2011

Printed in the United States of America

10 9 8 7 6 5 4 3 2 1

This book is printed on acid-free paper.

All links and Web addresses were checked and verified to be correct at the time of publication. Because of the dynamic nature of the Web, some addresses and links may have changed since publication and may no longer be valid.

Contents

Introduction

On July 14, 1969, in a special message to Congress, President Richard Nixon described drug abuse as "a serious national threat" to American life. Two years later, in June 1971, Nixon declared a "war on drugs," branding illegal drug use as "public enemy number one" in the United States.[1]

Over the next 40 years, six more presidents adopted Nixon's war analogy and tactics, spending billions of dollars each year to intercept illegal drug shipments and to imprison individuals caught selling, manufacturing, or using outlawed drugs. In May 2009 spokesmen for President Barack Obama announced that Washington would drop the "War on Drugs" label, emphasizing treatment over prosecution as a means of ending drug abuse—but the official campaign to seize illegal drugs goes on.[2]

Since 1973, the nation's frontline soldiers in this ongoing conflict have been agents of the Drug Enforcement Administration (DEA).

Throughout the War on Drugs—and long before it—Americans displayed confused and contradictory attitudes toward prohibition of various controlled substances. Sixty-three percent of those polled in February 2001 considered illegal drugs a "serious problem," while 27 percent called drug trafficking a "crisis" for America.[3] That view was contradicted, though, by surveys of illegal drug use nationwide, as is evident in the following U.S. government statistics:

- In the decade from 1988 to 1998, Americans spent between $39 billion and $77 billion per year on cocaine, and $10 billion to $22 billion per year on heroin.
- In 1998 hard-core cocaine users (those who took drugs more than 10 times per month) spent $191 a week on cocaine, and hard-core heroin users spent $214 a week on heroin.[4]

- Between 1988 and 1998, excluding imprisoned drug users, some 3.2 million to 3.9 million Americans were hard-core cocaine users, while 2.9 million to 6 million were occasional users. Another 630,000 to 980,000 Americans were hard-core heroin users, and 140,000 to 600,000 were occasional users.[5]
- A poll of high school seniors in 2006 found that 42.3 percent admitted using marijuana, 8.5 percent acknowledged using cocaine, and 1.4 percent said they used heroin.[6]
- The same poll found that 14 percent of 10th graders and 7 percent of 8th graders had smoked marijuana within the past month.[7]
- In 2005 25 percent of all high school students reported that someone had offered, sold, or given them illegal drugs on school property.[8]
- In 2007 19.9 million Americans aged 12 or older admitted using illegal drugs within the past month. During that year, 22.3 million persons aged 12 or older were diagnosed with substance dependence or abuse, including 3.7 million dependent on illegal drugs alone and 3.2 million who abused both drugs and alcohol.[9]

To halt that traffic, state and federal authorities spent $33,115,831,361 between January 1 and August 26, 2010. During the same seven months, 1,202,613 persons were arrested for drug violations and 7,605 were sentenced to prison.[10] During 2009, agents of the DEA alone arrested 30,567 drug-law violators nationwide.[11]

Illegal drug use also spawns crimes unrelated to simple possession, manufacture, or use of controlled substances. In 2004 18 percent of all federal prisoners and 17 percent of state prison inmates admitted committing their crimes to raise money for drugs. Among those convicted of property crimes (burglary, shoplifting, theft, etc.), the number increased to 30 percent of state inmates and 26 percent of federal prisoners. According to the Federal Bureau of Investigation (FBI), the United States suffered 794 drug-related murders in 2006. In the same year, 27 percent of all violent-crime victims reported that their attackers were under the influence of drugs or alcohol.[12]

Against all odds—risking their lives against violent drug syndicates and narco-terrorists, often obstructed by the very citizens who claim support for strict enforcement of America's drug laws—the men and women of the Drug Enforcement Administration pursue

The emblem of the Drug Enforcement Administration (DEA) is displayed at the United States embassy in Berlin, Germany. In addition to its 200-plus domestic offices, the DEA has more than 80 field offices in 62 foreign countries. *(Tim Brakemeier/dpa/Corbis)*

their sometimes thankless duty. *Drug Enforcement Administration* tells their story in chapters recounting the agency's history and its campaigns worldwide.

Chapter 1, "Drug Wars," charts the DEA's history and predecessor agencies, while detailing its modern mission.

Chapter 2, "Reefer Madness," reviews the federal war on marijuana—predating the creation of the DEA by four decades—and its progress today.

Chapter 3, "South of the Border," examines Mexico's role as the primary source of illegal drugs sold in America, and the brutal violence spawned by that traffic, which claimed 6,000 lives in 2008 alone.

Chapter 4, "Cocaine Cowboys," chronicles the DEA's long struggle against South American drug cartels and the violence of narco-terrorism.

Chapter 5, "Heroin Trails," surveys the global heroin trade and the DEA's efforts to halt it, at home and abroad.

Chapter 6, "Crystal Death," investigates the modern methamphetamine epidemic and the DEA's attempts to curb it.

Chapter 7, "Blood Money," follows DEA agents into another realm, pursuing criminals who hide and launder money for drug cartels and other wealthy criminals worldwide.

Chapter 8, "Fallen Soldiers," tells the stories of DEA agents killed in the line of duty since 1973.

Drug Wars

Washington, D.C.

On February 25, 2009, U.S. Attorney General Eric Holder Jr. and DEA Acting Administrator Michele Leonhart announced the arrest of 755 persons in three countries, coupled with the seizure of $59.1 million in cash and 23 tons of illegal narcotics. The international sweep, code-named "Operation Xcellerator," targeted members of Mexico's Sinaloa Cartel, a criminal organization responsible for smuggling heroin and other drugs worldwide.[1]

Launched in June 2007, Operation Xcellerator involved DEA agents, state and local police in nine U.S. states, as well as officers in Canada and Mexico. In addition to the arrests and cash seized, raiders also confiscated 26,400 pounds of cocaine, 16,000 pounds of marijuana, 1,200 pounds of methamphetamine, 18 pounds of heroin, and 1.3 million Ecstasy tablets. Other confiscated property, valued in excess of $6.5 million, included 149 vehicles, three aircraft, three boats, and 169 weapons.[2]

While the statistics were impressive, no one suggested that Operation Xcellerator had put the Sinaloa Cartel out of business. Cartel leader Joaquín Guzmán Loera remained at large, and was listed by *Forbes* magazine in March 2009 as the world's 701st richest man, with a personal fortune of $1 billion.[3] His agents are active throughout the world, and Mexico's drug war produced 9,800 murders between January 2008 and July 2009, with no end in sight.[4]

Attorney General Holder addressed that problem at the press conference announcing completion of Operation Xcellerator. "International drug trafficking organizations pose a sustained, serious threat to the safety and security of our communities," he said. "As the world grows smaller and international criminals step up their efforts to operate inside our borders, the Department of Justice will confront them head on to keep our communities safe."[5]

CONTROLLING SUBSTANCES

Federal laws governing "controlled substances" date from the first tax on whiskey, in 1791. That law sparked Pennsylvania's "Whiskey Rebellion" three years later, and Americans have introduced various restrictions on intoxicating drugs ever since.

In 1919 passage of the Eighteenth Amendment to the U.S. Constitution went a step further, banning alcoholic drinks nationwide as of January 16, 1920. The "dry" era known as Prohibition lasted until December 1933, creating an epic crime wave of smuggling, bootlegging, bribery, and gang warfare that ended with the creation of America's first national crime syndicate (a coalition of bootleggers and other gangsters formed to reduce bloodshed and increase profits from bootlegging, organized over time between 1927 and 1932). It was, in short, a spectacular failure.

DEA historians trace their agency's roots to the Treasury Department's Prohibition Unit, created in 1920 and renamed the Bureau of Prohibition in April 1927. While the Bureau of Prohibition's main focus was illegal liquor, its agents also pursued violators of America's limited federal drug laws. Four agents—Bert Gregory, James Williams, James Brown, and James Kerrigan—lost their lives in drug raids between 1922 and 1928.[6]

Drug enforcement duties were removed from the Bureau of Prohibition on June 14, 1930, and handed to the new Federal Bureau of Narcotics (FBN) led by Director Harry Anslinger. The FBN initially enforced two laws, the Harrison Narcotics Tax Act of December 1914, which regulated the importation and sale of opium and coca, and the Narcotic Drugs Import and Export Act of May 1922, which tightened restrictions of the 1914 law. In August 1937, thanks in large part to personal campaigning by Harry Anslinger, Congress passed the Marihuana Tax Act, imposing a five-year prison term on smugglers and dealers of marijuana or hashish.

Anslinger faced stiff opposition from FBI Director J. Edgar Hoover, who denied the existence of organized crime and complained that the FBN had copied his bureau's initials to gain publicity. Anslinger retired in 1962—the same year Hoover finally admitted the existence of the Mafia—and was replaced by Henry Giordano, a former pharmacist who led the FBN until August 1968, when it merged with the Food and Drug Administration's Bureau of Drug Abuse Control to form the new Bureau of Narcotics and Dangerous Drugs (BNDD). By then, six FBN agents had died in the line of duty during the agency's 38 years of pursuing drug smugglers.[7]

DEMAND REDUCTION PROGRAM

While the DEA's primary job is enforcement of federal drug laws, the agency's leaders understand that drug trafficking will never stop as long as a demand exists for controlled substances. With that in mind, the DEA's Demand Reduction Program strives to educate the public on adverse effects of drug abuse and the role played by illegal drugs in other crimes.

Launched in 1985, the Demand Reduction Program has established partnerships with other law enforcement agencies, as well as various civilian programs aimed at reducing public demand for illegal drugs. Thirty-one handpicked DEA agents serve as demand reduction coordinators (DRCs), based in communities across the country. The DEA lists the program's top priorities as: (1) providing timely intelligence to prevention and treatment partners; (2) helping the public, parents, and children understand the danger of drugs; and (3) presenting information on the damage drugs cause to non-users.[8]

Specific areas of emphasis for the Demand Reduction Program include the following:

Unlike the FBN, the BNDD was assigned to the Department of Justice, where its enforcement duties were not chiefly based on internal revenue statutes. New laws passed since Harry Anslinger convinced Congress to ban marijuana included the Opium Poppy Control Act of 1942 (banning unlicensed cultivation), the Durham-Humphrey Amendment of 1951 (defining prescription drugs and regulating their sale), the Boggs Act of 1951 (imposing mandatory prison sentences for drug-law violators), and the Narcotics Control Act of 1956 (increasing the 1951 penalties). By 1971 the busy BNDD had 1,500 agents and a budget of $43 million—14 times the FNB's maximum funding.[9] Drug-law violators murdered four BNDD agents between October 1970 and April 1973.[10]

- ★ *Anti-legalization education,* opposing various efforts to legalize (or "decriminalize") illicit drugs through a DEA publication titled "Speaking Out Against Drug Legalization," available at the agency's Web site.[11]
- ★ *Law enforcement training,* using DRCs to teach state and local police new ways of curbing drug use besides arresting violators and seizing illegal drugs. To that end, DRCs visit police academies and public schools, conduct training programs for officers involved in the Drug Abuse Resistance Education (D.A.R.E.) program, and present information to larger groups, such as the National Sheriffs' Association and the International Association of Chiefs of Police.
- ★ *Workplace education,* conducted with assistance from local Chambers of Commerce, to provide instruction on the damage caused by drugs each year, including workplace accidents and violence, absenteeism, and lost productivity amounting to billions of dollars.
- ★ *Community coalitions,* supported or created by the DEA, coordinating antidrug education at various levels in major cities such as Los Angeles, Dallas, and Richmond, Virginia.

Still, it was not enough. In January 1972, seven months after officially declaring war on drugs, President Richard Nixon created the Office of Drug Abuse Law Enforcement (ODALE), an agency of the Department of Justice, conceived to assist state and local governments with drug-law enforcement, while compelling addicts to seek rehabilitation. After 13 months of mixed results, in March 1973 Nixon signed "Reorganization Plan No. 2," merging ODALE and the BNDD into a single organization. Named the Drug Enforcement Administration, the new agency was formally established on July 1, 1973. It began with 1,470 agents and a budget of $74.9 million. Two years later, the DEA had 2,135 field agents and a budget of $140.9 million.[12]

MISSION IMPOSSIBLE?

The DEA's stated mission is "to enforce the controlled substances laws and regulations of the United States and bring to the criminal and civil justice system of the United States, or any other competent jurisdiction, those organizations and principal members of organizations, involved in the growing, manufacture, or distribution of controlled substances appearing in or destined for illicit traffic in the United States; and to recommend and support non-enforcement programs aimed at reducing the availability of illicit controlled substances on the domestic and international markets."[13]

But is that even possible, given the public appetite for drugs and the vast fortunes earned by those who manufacture and sell them? Statistics offer some evaluation of the breadth of the task. Between 1986 and 2009, DEA agents arrested 623,454 drug-law violators in America. During the same period, they also seized 3,156,743 pounds of cocaine, 31,719 pounds of heroin, 14,731,823 pounds of marijuana, 53,510 pounds of methamphetamine, and 146,629,079 dosage units of hallucinogens.[14]

All that, and still, optimistic government spokesmen admit that barely 30 percent of the illegal drugs imported into the Unites States each year are seized by all federal, state, and local law enforcement agencies combined. Some sources place the estimate as low as 10 percent.[15]

Drug enforcement in America is frustrating, expensive, and dangerous. Since the DEA's establishment in 1973, 59 agents have lost their lives in the line of duty, 15 of them slain by violent criminals.[16]

DRUG CZARS

America's Constitution forbids all "titles of nobility" in the United States, but politicians and journalists sometimes forget that basic rule when searching for dramatic phrases in a speech or news report.[17] The term *drug czar*—borrowing a royal title from the former monarch of imperial Russia—first appeared in October 1982, when a story published by United Press International reported that "Senators . . . voted 62-34 to establish a 'drug czar' who would have overall responsibility for U.S. drug policy."[18]

In fact, the "drug czar" title referred to Carlton Turner, named by President Ronald Reagan to lead the newly created Drug Abuse Policy Office, renamed the Office of National Drug Control Policy (ONDCP) in 1988. As stated on its Web site, the "principal purpose of ONDCP is to establish policies, priorities, and goals for the Nation's drug control program. To achieve this, ONDCP is charged with producing the National Drug Control Strategy. The Strategy directs the Nation's anti-drug efforts and establishes a program, a budget, and guidelines for cooperation among Federal, State, and local entities."[19]

In broad terms, the ONDCP's director supervises, coordinates, and evaluates all antidrug efforts carried out by the executive branch of the federal government, both domestic and foreign. In practice, the "drug czar" has little or no personal control of antidrug campaigns in the field, but serves primarily as an advisor to the president.

Some critics have objected to the "drug czar" label, both on constitutional grounds and for reasons of public relations, suggesting that it makes the government seem dictatorial. In January 2005 the General Accounting Office in Washington, D.C., formally declared that "use of the term 'Drug Czar' to describe the Director of the ONDCP does not constitute unlawful self-aggrandizement."[20]

THE DEA TODAY

The modern DEA's responsibilities include the following, as listed on the agency's Web site:

- Investigation and arrest of major drug-law violators who traffic in controlled substances across state lines or between the United States and foreign countries.
- Investigation and arrest of drug-dealing gangs or syndicates that terrorize local communities with acts of violence and intimidation.
- Seizure and forfeiture of any assets (vehicles, weapons, buildings, cash, jewelry, etc.) derived from, traceable to, or intended for use in illegal drug trafficking.
- Enforcement of the 1970 Comprehensive Drug Abuse and Control Act as it applies to the manufacture, distribution, and dispensing of legally produced controlled substances.
- Management of a national drug intelligence program enabling federal, state, local, and foreign officials to collect, analyze, and share intelligence related to illegal drug trafficking.
- Coordination with federal, state, local, and foreign officials of mutual drug enforcement efforts across jurisdictional lines, including non-enforcement activities such as crop eradication and substitution.
- Responsibility for the United States's share of all antidrug programs conducted in foreign countries, including liaison with the United Nations, Interpol, and other international law enforcement agencies, under direction of the Secretary of State and various U.S. ambassadors.[21]

The DEA is led by an administrator of drug enforcement, appointed by the president, who reports to the attorney general. The administrator's aides include a deputy administrator, a chief of operations, a chief inspector, and three assistant administrators for the agency's Operations Support, Intelligence, and Human Resources Divisions. DEA headquarters is located near the Pentagon, in Arlington, Virginia. The agency operates its own training academy, located on the U.S. Marine Corps Base at Quantico, Virginia, which also houses the more famous FBI Academy.

DEA agents simulate a raid in their Tactical Training Facility, part of the National Clandestine Laboratory Training and Research Facility at the DEA Training Academy in Quantico, Virginia. *(Tim Sloan/AFP/Getty Images)*

Applicants for jobs with the DEA are screened for security reasons, and to weed out any persons with a history of using "hard drugs." The agency explains that policy as follows: "Applicants who are found, through investigation or personal admission, to have experimented with or used narcotics or dangerous drugs, except those medically prescribed, will not be considered for employment with DEA. Exceptions to this policy may be made for applicants who admit to limited youthful and experimental use of marijuana. Such applicants may be considered for employment if there is no evidence of regular, confirmed usage and the full-field background investigation and results of the other steps in the process are otherwise favorable. Compliance with this policy is an essential requirement of the position."[22]

In addition to drug screening, applicants for service as DEA field agents, diversion investigators, and intelligence research specialists must also pass a polygraph ("lie detector") examination concerning drug use and other criminal behavior, prior to acceptance as recruits. DEA policy differs from that of the FBI, which relaxed its hiring standards for ex–drug abusers in October 2005.[23]

Once prospective agents complete their training at Quantico, they are dispersed among 21 domestic field divisions with 227 local officers, or sent off to one of the DEA's 86 foreign field offices in 62 other countries. The agency's 5,235 current agents are aided by a staff 5,300 support personnel.[24] The DEA's ongoing programs include the following:

- *Aviation,* dating from 1971, when the Bureau of Narcotics and Dangerous Drugs bought its first aircraft. By 1973 the program included 24 aircraft and 41 agents trained as pilots. Formerly assigned to the agency's Special Projects Division, in 1994 the Aviation Section achieved field division status as the Office of Aviation Operations (OA). Presently, the OA has approximately 100 aircraft and 125 agent-pilots, assigned to duties ranging from standard transportation to covert surveillance.[25] Since 1974, 11 DEA agents have died in job-related airplane crashes.[26]
- *Forensic Sciences,* maintaining a network of laboratories specifically designed to aid investigation and prosecution by analyzing confiscated drugs. Various tasks assigned to DEA forensic chemists include "signature programs" that monitor patterns of drug

At the DEA Training Academy in Quantico, Virginia, a DEA agent wears a full chemical suit in a room used to teach the methods of assessing an operational clandestine methamphetamine laboratory. *(Tim Sloan/AFP/Getty Images)*

trafficking through the identification of occluded (trapped) solvents in cocaine, heroin, methamphetamine, and methylenedioxymethamphetamine (ecstasy); the examination of logos and tablet characteristics of ecstasy and related "club drug" tablets; and the determination of the geographical or synthetic origins of cocaine, heroin, and methamphetamine. The DEA's Office of Forensic Sciences also publishes the quarterly *Microgram Journal* and a monthly *Microgram Bulletin,* designed to aid forensic chemists nationwide in the detection and analysis of suspected controlled substances.

- *Computer Forensics,* established in October 1994 "to recover information of probative value from computers and magnetic storage media." Since then, use of computers and related technology has expanded into every phase of modern law enforcement. Confiscated computers are scoured for incriminating evidence, even when seemingly damaged beyond repair. The unit's motto (referring to hard drives) is "If it spins then it can be read."[27] Data recovered from those sources may include bank account numbers; names and addresses of criminals; assets and financial activity, sales, and other business records; grid coordinates of clandestine landing strips; recipes for methamphetamine manufacture; plus e-mail and other incriminating correspondence.

o *Diversion Control,* assigned to stop the manufacture of illegal drugs and illicit diversion of prescription medicines. It deals with two distinct and separate problems: diversion of controlled chemicals and diversion of controlled pharmaceuticals. The first class of cases involves chemicals used to synthesize illegal drugs from raw coca and opium, or to manufacture synthetic drugs such as methamphetamine, LSD, and PCP. The second class involves pursuit of doctors, pharmacists, or licensed manufacturers who sell prescription drugs to addicts or illegal drug traffickers. Federal laws governing these areas include the Chemical Diversion and Trafficking Act of 1988, the Anabolic Steroid Control Act of 1991, the Comprehensive Methamphetamine Control Act of 1996, and the Methamphetamine Anti-Proliferation Act of 2000. The DEA and U.S. State Department also drafted Article 12 of the 1988 United Nations Convention Against Illicit Drug Traffic, which established global controls over 22 critical chemicals commonly diverted for the production of the major drugs of abuse.

o *Narcotics Registration,* a system that monitors access to various controlled substances by medical professionals, researchers, and manufacturers. All legitimate drug manufacturers, researchers, pharmacists, and persons licensed to prescribe drugs (doctors, dentists, nurse practitioners, etc.) have individual DEA numbers that may be revoked for any illicit activity, in addition to criminal prosecution.

o *High-Intensity Drug Trafficking Areas* (HIDTAs), a program authorized by the Anti–Drug Abuse Act of 1988 and assigned its present name in 1990, designed to disrupt the market for illegal drugs in the United States. As this book went to press, there were 32 recognized HIDTA headquarters, including 30 in the continental United

States, one in Hawaii, and one covering Puerto Rico and the U.S. Virgin Islands. All are regions known for high levels of illegal drug smuggling, manufacture, and abuse.[28]

- *Mobile Enforcement Teams* (METs), specialized teams dedicated to combating drug trafficking and drug-related urban violence in cooperation with local police. METs are scattered nationwide in the DEA's 21 field divisions, sometimes expanding their targets from big-city gangs to rural drug syndicates. Many state and local law enforcement agencies have copied the DEA by creating their own paramilitary units, often called "clandestine laboratory enforcement teams." All are patterned on traditional SWAT teams (Special Weapons *and* Tactics), with unique training and equipment required to raid drug labs filled with toxic and explosive chemicals.[29]

- *Foreign Cooperative Investigations,* initiated by the FBN in 1949, when Harry Anslinger recognized that nearly all opium, heroin, cocaine, and hashish—along with large quantities of marijuana—is imported to the United States from foreign countries. Cooperation with other nations was largely informal until 1976, when Washington imposed specific rules requiring DEA cooperation with host nations and banning agents from arresting suspects abroad. Today, agents assigned to the DEA's field offices in 58 countries worldwide perform different law enforcement functions. They include the following:

  1. *Bilateral investigations,* sharing information and joining in antidrug campaigns conducted by host nations, including drug seizures and interrogation of suspects.
  2. *Institution building,* defined as assisting foreign police departments—such as the Colombian National Police, Mexico's Federal Investigations Agency, and Russia's Federal Security Service—with efforts designed to intercept illegal drugs before they reach America.
  3. *International training,* offered to selected foreign law enforcement officers, both in their native countries and at the DEA's academy in Quantico, Virginia.
  4. *Intelligence gathering,* required for any successful campaign against drug traffickers or any other element of organized

crime. An early example was the El Paso (Texas) Intelligence Center, created in 1974, which presently coordinates enforcement programs of the DEA; FBI; Secret Service; U.S. Marshals Service; Bureau of Alcohol, Tobacco, Firearms and Explosives (ATF); Department of Homeland Security; Customs & Border Protection; Immigration and Customs Enforcement; U.S. Coast Guard; National Drug Intelligence Center; Internal Revenue Service; U.S. Department of the Interior; Department of Defense; Texas Department of Public Safety; Texas Air National Guard; and the El Paso County Sheriff's Office. A broader-ranging program, the Joint Information Coordination Centers, provides computer hardware and software to 20 foreign host countries located in Central America, South America, and the Caribbean.[30]

5. *Foreign-deployed Advisory and Support Teams* (FASTs), created in April 2005 to help curb a rapid increase in heroin production following America's invasion of Afghanistan in 2001. Five FAST groups presently exist, with two serving 120 days on active duty in Afghanistan, while three continue training in Quantico, Virginia, and await rotation to the field. In Afghanistan, their assignments include identifying, targeting, investigating, and disrupting or dismantling drug networks, in cooperation with the Afghan Special Narcotics Force, created in 2003.[31]

Reefer
Madness

Washington, D.C.

On April 13, 2000, DEA spokesmen announced the conclusion of "Operation Green Air," which dismantled a marijuana-smuggling network that imported the illegal drug from Mexico, and then shipped it nationwide with help from employees of the Federal Express (FedEx) courier service. The operation climaxed with more than 100 arrests nationwide; 25 corrupt FedEx employees were among those arrested. Raiders also seized $4.2 million in cash and 34,000 pounds of marijuana.[1]

Behind the drug network was Baja California's Tijuana Cartel, a smuggling syndicate founded by Miguel Félix Gallardo and run by his seven sons, the Arellano Félix brothers, since the gang's creator was jailed in 1989. Recognized as "one of the biggest and most violent criminal groups in Mexico," the Tijuana Cartel has been linked to numerous murders.[2] One incident, on September 17, 1998, left 18 persons dead in Ensenada. In April 2008 14 gunmen died and eight were wounded in a Tijuana shootout between members of the Arellano Félix gang and killers from the rival Sinaloa Cartel.

In the conspiracy disrupted by Operation Green Air, cartel smugglers brought marijuana from Mexico to Los Angeles, where FedEx employees sent the drugs off in overnight parcels to accomplices in Connecticut, Florida, Georgia, Massachusetts, New Jersey, New York, and Pennsylvania. Launched in 1998, the network had shipped 4,000 packages of marijuana—a total of 121 tons valued at $145 million—by the time Green Air's arrests shut it down.[3]

Announcing Operation Green Air's success, Attorney General Janet Reno told reporters, "Today we have taken another major step in our fight against drug trafficking. Law enforcement's overnight delivery to the American people is safer streets for our children."[4]

THE ROOTS OF "GRASS"

Marijuana belongs to the genus of flowering plants named *Cannabis,* cultivated for thousands of years for various uses. Its fibers—known as "hemp"—have been used since ancient times to manufacture rope and writing paper. Cannabis also contains the chemical tetrahydrocannabinol (THC), which produces an intoxicating high when smoked or eaten.

Despite ongoing debate and confusion, science recognizes at least three species of cannabis. The most common is marijuana (*Cannabis sativa*), also known as "reefer," "pot," "grass," "weed," and by many other street names. Hashish (*Cannabis indica*) is native to Central Asia, while a third and milder species, *Cannabis ruderalis,* normally grows in eastern Europe and Russia.

The first known mention of cannabis is found in the world's oldest medical text, the *Shen Nung Pen Ts'ao Ching* ("Divine Husbandman's Classic of Materia Medica"), published in China around 2737 B.C., which describes cannabis as a "superior" herb. Roman physician Pedanius Dioscorides (A.D. 40–90) described medicinal uses of cannabis in his work *De Materia Medica.*[5]

Official views of cannabis have varied through the ages. Muhammad, the founder of Islam (570–632 A.D.), condemned drinking alcohol but permitted smoking of hashish. Pope Innocent VIII (1432–1492) banned hashish-smoking by Christians soon after taking office in 1484. British colonial authorities *required* North American colonists to grow cannabis during the 17th and 18th centuries, and future president George Washington was one of Virginia's leading hemp farmers, ordering his gardener to "make the most of the Indian hemp seed, and sow it everywhere." Those crops were theoretically confined to making rope or paper, but some historians suggest that the plants were also used to produce recreational drugs.[6]

Francisco Javier Arellano Félix, former kingpin of the Tijuana Cartel, arrives in San Diego in August 2006. After pleading not guilty to federal charges of moving tons of cocaine and marijuana along the California-Mexico border, he pled guilty in September 2007 to running a criminal enterprise and laundering money. He was sentenced to life in prison. *(AP Photo/Department of Justice)*

EARLY LEGISLATION

Cannabis remained a legal substance in America through the early 20th century. Hashish was served at the 1876 American Centennial Exposition in Philadelphia, two decades before the term *marijuana* was coined by supporters of Mexican revolutionary leader Pancho Villa

(1878–1923), around 1895. In 1912 representatives of 46 nations signed the Hague Convention for the Suppression of Opium and Other Drugs, but while they agreed to limits on the manufacture and sale of opium, morphine, heroin, and cocaine, cannabis was not included.[7]

California and Utah were the first American states to ban marijuana, in 1915. Four years later, ratification of the Constitution's Eighteenth Amendment encouraged some states to ban intoxicants other than alcohol. Texas outlawed cannabis in 1919; Louisiana, Nevada, Oregon, and Washington followed suit in 1923; and New York banned marijuana in 1927.[8]

Today, some historians suggest that the early anti-marijuana laws were racist in nature, mainly directed at Mexican Americans in western states. Before the final vote on cannabis in 1919, one Texas state legislator declared, "All Mexicans are crazy, and this stuff [marijuana] is what makes them crazy."[9]

"REEFER MADNESS"

Enter Harry Anslinger, appointed to lead the Federal Bureau of Narcotics in 1930. Current federal laws applied only to opiates and coca derivatives, but Anslinger quickly launched a personal campaign to outlaw cannabis nationwide. In 1931, when hemp producers advertised their product as America's next billion-dollar crop, Anslinger denounced new mechanical harvesters as ineffective. Later, supported by newspaper magnate William Randolph Hearst and President Franklin Roosevelt, Anslinger went further, condemning marijuana as a menace to society.

During 1936 and 1937, Anslinger and his FBN agents joined religious groups and Hollywood studios to produce a series of films depicting cannabis as a drug that drives youngsters insane. The most famous such film was *Reefer Madness* (1936), released in some markets under the title *Tell Your Children*. That film, directed by Louis Gasnier, portrays drugged teenagers running wild in a rampage of hit-and-run accidents, rape, murder, and suicide. During the same year, producer Dwain Esper released *Marihuana, the Devil's Weed*, also known as *Marihuana, the Weed with Roots in Hell!* In 1937 Elmer Clifton directed *Assassin of Youth*, also known as *The Marihuana Menace*. ("Marihuana" was the standard English spelling of *marijuana* in the early 20th century, since the letter *j* in Spanish is pronounced as *h*.) While considered

OUT OF AFRICA

While U.S. media reports stress marijuana as a homegrown drug or one imported from Latin America, Africa has emerged as a major alternative source, transit territory, and consumer market. Nations heavily involved in the traffic include

★ *South Africa,* described by some observers as the world's leading cannabis (or *dagga*) producer, though much of the crop is consumed in-country, by residents and an increasing number of "cannabis tourists." Drug seizures and arrests persistently fail to keep pace with cultivation and illegal importation. Some outside observers criticized President Thabo Mbeki, who ruled South Africa from 1999 until his forced resignation in September 2008, noting that cannabis seizures in Johannesburg declined from 27,122 pounds in 1998 to 1,439 pounds in 1999, while available supplies increased. During the same period, cocaine seizures dropped from 1,364 pounds to 196 pounds. Meanwhile, various sources describe cannabis plantations spanning 86,000 to 198,000 acres.[10]

★ *Lesotho,* an impoverished nation where the average worker earns less than $1,300 per year, supports a thriving traffic in cannabis (called *matekoane* in the Sesotho language), exporting much of its crop to neighboring South Africa. Known for cultivating cannabis since 1550, farmers use the drug to treat minor ailments and export their surplus to supplement minimal income, averaging five harvests per year. Officials blame "foreigners" for the problem, as well as for more recent proliferation of cocaine and LSD.[11]

★ *Algeria,* a primary supplier of cannabis to European markets. Authorities seized 40,000 pounds of hashish and 900,000 hallucinogenic tablets between January and September 2008, arresting 2,399 suspects (including 17 foreigners). Still, the traffic thrives, with hashish cultivation centered in mountainous regions controlled by rebel Armed Islamic

(continues)

(continued)

Group of Algeria guerrillas. Algeria's chaotic and violent political climate, coupled with its Mediterranean seacoast and 4,200 miles of land borders, make drug interdiction a difficult task, at best.[12]

★ *Morocco,* Algeria's next-door neighbor, remains a prime cannabis producer and exporter, despite erratic crackdowns on the traffic. In August 2008 authorities seized two tons of hashish from one dealer and destroyed 6,758 acres of cultivated cannabis, without putting a dent in the trade. Joint operations with Spanish police, beginning in November 2008, produced more "record" seizures and multiple arrests, while the flow of drugs to Europe continued unabated.[13]

★ *Nigeria,* another major cannabis producer, despite the best efforts of its National Drug Law Enforcement Agency (NDLEA), operating since 1990. Widespread corruption persists, exemplified by the December 2007 arrest of former NDLEA commander Abdullahi Bayawo on charges of smuggling cocaine. Customers worldwide consume Nigerian cannabis—and now grow their own, from seeds sold on the Internet.[14]

★ *Democratic Republic of the Congo,* ranked as another of Africa's largest cannabis producers (mostly for domestic consumption). Pervasive corruption and loose regulation of banks makes the country a prime money-laundering center.[15]

★ *Kenya,* where longtime cannabis cultivation for domestic use has expanded into a lucrative export trade. Authorities acknowledge more than 3,700 acres under cultivation today, with smaller crops of opium poppies and much larger farms producing *khat* (a plant with stimulant properties grown in many parts of Africa and listed by the DEA as a controlled substance since 1993).[16]

While the DEA has offices in all of these African nations—and 13 others—its success in preventing drug shipments abroad relies on cooperation from local authorities, who are sometimes in league with drug traffickers.[17]

laughable today, such films had a dramatic impact on American audiences during the Great Depression.

Harry Anslinger also kept a "gore file" at FBN headquarters, filled with media and police reports of violent crimes that he linked to marijuana. Those, in turn, were used to produce articles for *American Magazine* and other publications in the 1930s, which Anslinger co-authored with Courtney Ryley Cooper (whose semi-fictional stories also promoted J. Edgar Hoover's "G-men"). One such article, titled "Marijuana, Assassin of Youth," includes this description of a supposed cannabis-related crime:

> An entire family was murdered by a youthful addict in Florida. When officers arrived at the home, they found the youth staggering about in a human slaughterhouse. With an axe he had killed his father, mother, two brothers, and a sister. He seemed to be in a daze . . . He had no recollection of having committed the multiple crime. The officers knew him ordinarily as a sane, rather quiet young man; now he was pitifully crazed. They sought the reason. The boy said that he had been in the habit of smoking something which youthful friends called "muggles," a childish name for marijuana.[18]

Soon after *American Magazine* published that article, on August 2, 1937, Congress passed the Marihuana Tax Act, banning the sale of marijuana without a special tax stamp from the U.S. Internal Revenue Service. Since no such stamps existed, then or later, marijuana trafficking became a federal crime, punishable by a maximum sentence of five years in prison and a $2,000 fine. The law remained in effect until 1970, when it was declared unconstitutional by the U.S. Supreme Court.

American concerns changed somewhat after World War II, from fears of Depression-era "crime waves" to worry over Russia's "Red Menace." Harry Anslinger changed with the times, dropping his claim that marijuana provoked violent crimes, claiming instead that it made smokers so relaxed they might not resist a communist invasion.

Congress responded as Anslinger hoped, passing the Boggs Act on November 2, 1951. The new law lumped cannabis together with heroin and cocaine, dictating mandatory prison terms for possession or sale of all three drugs: two to five years for a first offense; five to 10 years on a second conviction; and 10 to 20 years on a third charge, each sentence accompanied by a $2,000 fine.

Still, the prohibitionists were not satisfied. Four and a half years later, Congress passed the Narcotics Control Act, signed into law by President Dwight Eisenhower on July 15, 1956. That law left the 1951 penalties for drug possession intact, but added mandatory terms for selling banned drugs: five years for a first offense, 10 years for each additional conviction or for any adult caught selling drugs to a minor. Fines on each charge were increased tenfold, to $20,000, and parole was forbidden to repeat offenders.

CHANGING TIMES

The DEA still enforces the laws passed in the 1950s, but America's attitude toward marijuana has changed over time. The 1960s and early 1970s saw widespread expansion of cannabis use among hippies, college students, antiwar protesters, and U.S. soldiers who got their first taste of illegal drugs in Vietnam. Oregon considered legalizing marijuana in 1973, and Alaska approved possession of up to one ounce in 1975. Ignoring that state legislation, DEA agents continued performing their duty under federal law. Alaskan lawmakers changed their minds and banned marijuana once more in 1990.[19]

Various presidents also seemed conflicted in their views on marijuana. President Gerald Ford denounced cannabis in 1976, but his son admitted smoking it. Ford's successor, Jimmy Carter, suggested legalization in August 1977, but failed to achieve it. President Ronald Reagan condemned marijuana in 1984, while his wife launched a campaign urging American youth to "Just Say No" if they were offered drugs. President Bill Clinton admitted sampling marijuana in college, but claimed that he "didn't inhale." His calls for legalization in the 1990s brought no result from Congress. President George W. Bush dodged questions concerning his alleged drug use in college, and spokesmen for the Food and Drug Administration declared that "marijuana is the equivalent of heroin and cocaine."[20]

Through all of the confusion and mixed messages, DEA agents pursued their primary duty of enforcing federal laws as they are

MEDICAL MARIJUANA

"Medical marijuana" refers to any use of cannabis or synthetic THC prescribed or recommended by physicians to relieve symptoms of various diseases or medical treatments, such as the harsh side effects of chemotherapy used to fight cancer. It may be administered in various forms and doses: by smoking

(continues)

DEA agents remove marijuana plants from a medical marijuana dispensary in June 2005. The DEA shifted its policy in 2009 and no longer raids state-approved marijuana dispensaries. *(AP Photo/Ben Margot)*

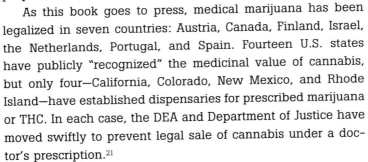

(continued)

or vaporization, by drinking or eating extracts, and by taking synthetic THC pills.

Modern applications of cannabis documented in medical journals worldwide include treatment for arthritis, asthma, glaucoma, nausea, inflammatory bowel disorders (Crohn's disease and ulcerative colitis), migraine headaches, digestive diseases, epilepsy, hypertension (high blood pressure), Parkinson's disease, sickle-cell disease, appetite loss and unintended weight loss, various symptoms of multiple sclerosis and spinal cord injuries, Tourette syndrome, sleep apnea, and many other serious disorders. The problem lies in convincing politicians and police that cannabis may ever serve a useful purpose.

As this book goes to press, medical marijuana has been legalized in seven countries: Austria, Canada, Finland, Israel, the Netherlands, Portugal, and Spain. Fourteen U.S. states have publicly "recognized" the medicinal value of cannabis, but only four—California, Colorado, New Mexico, and Rhode Island—have established dispensaries for prescribed marijuana or THC. In each case, the DEA and Department of Justice have moved swiftly to prevent legal sale of cannabis under a doctor's prescription.[21]

American policy makers remain sharply divided on the question of medical marijuana. In March 2004 former U.S. Surgeon General Joycelyn Elders said, "The evidence is overwhelming that marijuana can relieve certain types of pain, nausea, vomiting and other symptoms caused by such illnesses as multiple sclerosis, cancer and AIDS—or by the harsh

written. Between 1986 and 2009, the agency seized approximately 7 million tons of marijuana nationwide, a haul excluding all the tons captured by state or local police, the Coast Guard, Border Patrol, and U.S. Customs agents.[22] In 2007 alone, 47.4 percent of all American drug arrests—872,720 out of 1,841,182—involved marijuana. And

drugs sometimes used to treat them. And it can do so with remarkable safety. Indeed, marijuana is less toxic than many of the drugs that physicians prescribe every day."[23]

Opponents of medical marijuana often call for "more study," but some—like John Walters, director of the Office of National Drug Control Policy from 2001 to 2009—claim any use of cannabis is dangerous. In March 2002 he said, "Smoked marijuana damages the brain, heart, lungs, and immune system. It impairs learning and interferes with memory, perception, and judgment. Smoked marijuana contains cancer-causing compounds and has been implicated in a high percentage of automobile crashes and workplace accidents."[24]

Andrea Barthwell, former deputy director of the ONDCP, also claims that medical marijuana endangers children. In February 2004 she said, "Children entering drug abuse treatment routinely report that they heard that 'pot is medicine' and, therefore, believed it to be good for them."[25]

The federal view of medical marijuana apparently changed with the election of President Barack Obama. During the 2008 election campaign, he told reporters, "My attitude is if the science and the doctors suggest that the best palliative care and the way to relieve pain and suffering is medical marijuana, then that's something I'm open to." A month after Obama's inauguration, in February 2009, new Attorney General Eric Holder Jr. announced that the DEA would no longer raid state-approved cannabis dispensaries. "What the president said during the campaign . . . will be consistent with what we will be doing here in law enforcement," Holder said. "What he said during the campaign . . . is now American policy."[26]

although Hollywood fiction portrays the War on Drugs as a battle with sinister "kingpins," 88.8 percent of those jailed for marijuana violations (775,137 defendants) were arrested for possession without intent to sell. Those figures had increased from 734,497 marijuana arrests in 2000, when 646,042 persons were charged with simple possession.[27]

None of it seems to deter drug users. In addition to cannabis smuggled from foreign countries, vast supplies are grown in the United States. A government report issued in 2006 described marijuana as America's leading cash crop.[28] In August of that same year, the United Nations Office on Drugs and Crime declared that:

> Cannabis remains by far the most commonly used drug in the world. An estimated 162 million people used cannabis in 2004, equivalent to some 4 percent of the global population age 15–64. In relative terms, cannabis use is most prevalent in Oceania, followed by North America and Africa. While Asia has the lowest prevalence expressed as part of the population, in absolute terms it is the region that is home to some 52 million cannabis users, more than a third of the estimated total. The next largest markets, in absolute terms, are Africa and North America.[29]

As that report went to press, America's National Institute on Drug Policy addressed the domestic pot problem, reporting that "Marijuana appears to be readily available to almost all 12th graders; in 2005 86% reported that they think it would be 'very easy' or 'fairly easy' for them to get it—almost twice the number who reported ever having used it (45%). After marijuana, 12th-grade students indicated that amphetamines are among the easiest drugs to obtain (51%)."[30]

Clearly, the marijuana "menace" remains unresolved. As dedicated law enforcement officers, DEA agents follow orders and pursue their duties, leaving elected politicians to decide the issues of morality and public policy.

South of the Border

Mexico City, Mexico

Drug arrests occur daily in Mexico, but few create the public controversy that erupted on January 24, 2009, when Mexican authorities announced the climax of "Operation Clean House," aimed at ridding the government of corrupt officials. The dozen suspects jailed that day were all prominent members of President Felipe Calderón's government, including former federal police commissioner Victor Gerardo Garay and ex-prosecutor Noé Ramírez Mandujano. Both were charged with selling information to Mexico's notorious Sinaloa Cartel, which permitted the gang to dodge arrests and raids.[1]

DEA spokesmen estimate that traffickers smuggle drugs valued at $15 billion to $20 billion across the U.S.-Mexico border each year, protecting their pipelines by bribing officials at every level, from local police to heads of state. Agent Oscar Granados Salero, speaking for Mexico's Federal Investigative Agency, told reporters, "Whenever we were trying to serve arrest warrants, they were already waiting for us, and a lot of colleagues lost their lives that way." Noé Ramírez stood accused of taking $450,000 in bribes from the Sinaloa Cartel, while other officials received similar payoffs.[2]

Embarrassed by scandals that had forced the dismantling of whole police departments during recent years, President Calderón vowed that a "new generation of police" led by Safety Secretary Genaro Garcia Luna would stamp out corruption, but many observers were openly skeptical.[3] They noted that police in Mexico receive small salaries, and that those who reject bribes are frequently murdered. Robert Orduna, chief of police for Ciudad Juárez, resigned in February 2009, after drug traffickers threatened to kill one officer for every 48 hours that Orduna stayed on the job.[4] On July 11, 2009, alone, cartel gunmen killed five officers and wounded 18 more in eight Mexican cities.[5]

OPEN DOORS

Established by treaty in 1848, Mexico's border with the United States spans 1,950 miles from San Diego, California, on the west to Browns-ville, Texas, on the east. Legitimate commercial traffic flows in both directions, through 32 border towns located in the U.S. states of Cali-fornia, Arizona, New Mexico, and Texas, facing the Mexican states of Baja California, Sonora, Chihuahua, Coahuila, Nuevo León, and Tam-aulipas. Between towns, there lies open desert.[6]

Open trading aside, the Mexican border constitutes a major gap in America's national security. Mexican officials illegally crossed the bor-der 253 times between 1996 and 2006, but that figure pales in compari-son to the crossings made by drug traffickers.[7] In 1990 DEA spokesmen estimated that 80 percent of all cocaine entering the United States came through Mexico, a figure that increased to 90 percent—300 tons per year—by 2007.[8] At the same time, Mexican smugglers furnished 80 per-cent of the methamphetamine sold to American addicts and imported 242,000 pounds of marijuana each year.[9]

Decades of official bungling and corruption seemed about to end in December 2006, when President Calderón committed 25,000 troops to Mexico's war on drugs, scoring some apparent victories. By June 2008, Mexican authorities had made 5,800 arrests and intercepted 2,900 tons of marijuana and 24 tons of cocaine, costing drug cartels an estimated $20 billion. The downside was a swift increase in violence, claiming 1,400 lives. The list of murder victims included 450 soldiers and police officers.[10]

Clearly, America cannot win its own drug war while the Mexican border remains open to smugglers, but closing that border—and the airspace above it—seems to be impossible.

OPERATION TAR PIT

Between 1995 and 1998, 85 residents of Chimayo, New Mexico, died from injections of high-purity black tar heroin imported from Nayarit, Mexico. Later, the same drugs killed addicts in several other cities.[11] Those deaths prompted the DEA and FBI to launch "Operation Tar Pit," targeting Mexican heroin smugglers and their American clients nationwide.

The first arrests in Operation Tar Pit were made in Albuquerque, New Mexico, where agents jailed 33 suspects in October 1999. By June 2000, when the campaign was completed, a total of 249 defendants had been charged on various felony counts, in 12 cities ranging from Nashville, Tennessee, to Anchorage, Alaska, and the Hawaiian Islands. The Hawaiian raids bagged 28 suspects and climaxed with seizure of an orchid farm used as a front for drug smuggling. Other arrests were made in Alabama, Arizona, California, Colorado, Georgia, Illinois, Kentucky, Michigan, Minnesota, Nevada, New Jersey, Ohio, Oregon, Pennsylvania, and West Virginia. Raiders also seized 64 pounds of high-purity heroin, 10 weapons, and $304,450 in cash.[12]

Announcing the results of Operation Tar Pit, Attorney General Janet Reno told the media, "This operation is a classic illustration of how drug law enforcement works best—federal law enforcement agencies working cooperatively, one with the other and with state and local authorities and working in combination with the efforts of the prevention and treatment initiatives in the community."[13]

Guilty pleas on Operation Tar Pit charges began in Los Angeles, where 15 suspects were arrested. In August 2001 Oscar Hernandez and his wife, Marina Lopez, pled guilty to charges of possessing heroin with intent to distribute. Hernandez faced a maximum 100-year sentence, while Lopez faced a 20-year term.[14]

MURDER AND MAGIC

One of the strangest border traffickers on record is Adolfo Constanzo (1962–1989), born in Miami to a Puerto Rican mother and schooled from childhood in the practices of *palo mayombe,* a form of Afro-Caribbean black magic related to voodoo. At age 22, Constanzo moved to Mexico City and recruited a gang of disciples who revered him as *El Padrino* ("the Godfather"). He performed ritual "cleansings" for leaders of the drug-dealing Calzado family, then sacrificed them to his gods in 1987 and seized control of their network.

Moving his base of operations to Matamoros, across the border from Brownsville, Texas, Constanzo lured more followers who apparently believed that human sacrifice would make them both invisible and bulletproof. If that failed, Constanzo's cult was protected by corrupt police, including Salvador Garcia (chief of drug investigations for the Federal Judicial Police) and Florentino Ventura (head of Interpol's office in Mexico City).

Constanzo's luck ran out in March 1989, when his cult sacrificed an American college student kidnapped while on his spring break. The resultant investigation led officers to Constanzo's ranch near Matamoros, where they unearthed 15 mutilated bodies. Constanzo died in a shootout with Mexico City police on May 6, 1989, leaving 14 cult members to face trial for murder.[15]

CARTELS UNITED

Today, the Mexican drug trade is dominated by powerful cartels (combinations), which battle for control of the lucrative illegal industry. They include the following:

- The *Tijuana Cartel,* founded by Miguel Félix Gallardo (then the Guadalajara Cartel), has been run by his sons and nephews since his 1989 imprisonment for murdering DEA agent Enrique Camarena. Known as an extremely violent group, the Tijuana Cartel has fought pitched battles with its rivals, which inspired the Oscar-winning movie *Traffic* in 2000. Based in Baja California, the Tijuana Cartel operates in 15 Mexican states and ships its drugs all over the world.[16]

- The *Juárez Cartel* is based in Ciudad Juárez (across the border from El Paso, Texas), with operations in 21 Mexican states.[17] Amado Carrillo Fuentes led the cartel until his death, during plastic surgery, in 1997. (In his final days, Fuentes was on the run from Mexican and U.S. authorities; he underwent plastic surgery so he would not be recognizable.) Under his leadership, the cartel shipped 50 percent of all drugs sent from Mexico to the United States, earning an estimated $200 million per week.[18] Since 2005, Juárez Cartel

A U.S. Immigration and Customs Enforcement agent looks down a shaft of a tunnel that leads from the United States into Mexico in January 2006. DEA agents arrested Mexican drug lord Francisco Javier Arellano Félix, a leader of the major drug gang (the Tijuana Cartel) responsible for digging these elaborate tunnels to smuggle drugs under the U.S. border. *(AP Photo/Denis Poroy, File)*

members have called their organization the Golden Triangle Alliance, referring to operations in the states of Chihuahua, Durango, and Sinaloa.

o The *Sinaloa Cartel* operates in 17 Mexican states, smuggling a variety of drugs, including homegrown marijuana, Colombian cocaine, and "China white" heroin from Southeast Asia.[19] Leader Joaquín Guzmán Loera was imprisoned in 1993, but he escaped in 2001 and remains at large today. Eight years after his escape, *Forbes* magazine listed Guzmán among the world's richest people, with a personal fortune of $1 billion.[20] DEA spokesmen say that the Sinaloa Cartel now belongs to Mexico's Golden Triangle Alliance.

o The *Gulf Cartel,* founded in the 1970s by Juan Nepomuceno Guerra, operates in 13 Mexican states.[21] This group is a deadly rival of the Sinaloa Cartel. It has responded to the formation of the Golden Triangle Alliance by joining the Tijuana Cartel in a new combination, called "The Federation." The Gulf Cartel's private army, known as Los Zetas, recruits former soldiers and police officers to perform contract murders. In September 2008, DEA agents and other officers jailed more than 500 Gulf Cartel associates in the United States, Mexico, and Italy. The raiders also seized $60.1 million in cash, 36,764 pounds of cocaine, 1,039 pounds of methamphetamine, 19 pounds of heroin, 51,258 pounds of marijuana, 176 vehicles, and 167 weapons.[22] In February 2010 Los Zetas and the Gulf Cartel parted ways; they are now enemies.

o The *Beltrán-Leyva Cartel* is led by five brothers once allied with the Sinaloa Cartel who switched sides to work with the Gulf Cartel and Los Zetas after Alfredo Beltrán Leyva's arrest in January 2008. In March 2009, Mexican authorities offered a reward of 30 million pesos ($2.1 million) for information leading to the arrest of the remaining Beltrán-Leyva brothers and their top aides, Sergio Villarreal Barragán and Édgar Valdéz Villareal.[23] So far, there have been no takers.

o The *Michoacán Cartel,* also known as La Familia ("The Family"), is presently led by Servando Gomez. DEA investigators say that La Familia was once part of the Gulf Cartel, but broke away to run its own smuggling operations in 2006. That September, masked men

Mexican federal police officers escort Alfredo Beltrán Leyva, known as "El Mochomo," upon his arrival at the Mexico City airport in January 2008. *(AP Photo/Eduardo Verdugo)*

who called themselves "Family" members tossed five human heads onto the dance floor of a nightclub in Uruapan. Former cartel leader Alberto Espinoza Barron was jailed in December 2008, following a hand-grenade attack that killed eight people and injured more than 100 in Morelia.[24] In July 2009 cartel members tortured and killed 12 Mexican federal agents.[25]

WHOSE LAW AND ORDER?

Crime syndicates cannot survive without protection from corrupt public officials. Despite assistance from the DEA, drug-related corruption in Mexico remains a serious problem. President Vicente Fox Quesada (president of Mexico from 2000 to 2006) disbanded the graft-riddled Federal Judicial Police in October 2001, replacing it with the new Federal Investigations Agency (AFI), but that failed to solve the problem. In December 2005 Mexico's attorney general announced that 1,500 of the AFI's 7,000 officers were under investigation for criminal activity, with 457 already indicted.[26] Rodolfo de la Guardia García, second in command of the AFI, was arrested in November 2008 for leaking information to the Sinaloa Cartel. President Calderón disbanded the AFI in May 2009, replacing it with the Ministerial Federal Police.

Still, corruption continues at all levels of Mexican government and law enforcement. In December 2006 President Calderón ordered ballistics tests on all police weapons, to see if any were used in drug murders. In April 2007 more than 100 state police officers in Nuevo León were suspended for taking bribes. Two months later, President Calderón fired 284 federal police commanders, ordering regular drug and polygraph tests for those who remained.[27] Operation Clean House followed in January 2009, including the arrest of Rodolfo de la Guardia García, ex-director of Mexico's Interpol office. Despite such efforts, virtually no one believes that a true "clean house" has been achieved.

THE *OTHER* DRUG WAR

While DEA agents and some Mexican police work to crush drug cartels, the cartels continue battling one another. Drug trafficking was relatively peaceful until 1989, when Mexico's Institutional Revolutionary Party lost power and its rising opposition severed government ties with large drug syndicates. Skirmishing continued through the 1990s, but the violence has turned into wholesale slaughter since President Fox fielded troops against smugglers in 2000. According to the Mexican attorney general, cartel assassins killed 10,475 victims between December 2006 and April 2009. Ten percent of the dead were police or other public servants.[28]

Frontline soldiers in the cartel wars are members of Los Zetas, fighting for The Federation, and Los Negros, serving the Golden Triangle Alliance. Both consist of former soldiers and police, equipped with modern military weapons, including heavy machine guns, grenade launchers, and ground-to-air missiles. Their major battlegrounds include the following locations:

- *Nuevo Laredo,* where cartel gunmen kill police and journalists, as well as one another. Kidnapping gangs in the city abducted 60 American citizens—20 of whom are still missing—between 2003 and 2007.[29] Some sources claim that local fighting ended in 2007, but the city still suffered 55 drug-related murders in 2008.[30]
- *Guerrero,* a state on Mexico's southern Pacific coast, where cartel assassins killed Acapulco's police chief and narrowly missed the state's attorney general in April 2006. Los Zetas also beheaded several victims that year. In March 2007 they left one headless body with a "Z" carved on its chest as a grisly signature. An Acapulco shootout in June 2009 left two soldiers and 15 cartel gunmen dead.[31]
- *Michoacán,* adjacent to Guerrero, where the large cartel alliances battle one another and the Colima Cartel, led by the Amezcua brothers (known as "the Kings of Methamphetamine"). During July 2006 alone, three shootouts claimed eight lives, and a member of the Sinaloa Cartel was ambushed by rivals who shot him 100 times. Antidrug efforts focus on Apatzingan, where residents accuse Mexican soldiers of human rights violations.[32] In July 2009 10 local policemen were arrested for killing 12 federal agents.[33]
- *Ciudad Juárez,* where the death toll includes hundreds of women and girls, in addition to drug cartel gunmen. Shootouts between rival traffickers claimed 250 lives in March 2009 alone, prompting President Calderón to flood the city with 2,000 soldiers and federal agents. The previous month, during a single day, cartel assassins

killed 17 people, burned dozens of buildings, and kidnapped a relative of an American congressman.[34]

Because gun sales are restricted in Mexico, the cartels fight with weapons smuggled from other nations. According to the ATF, at least 22,848 guns were smuggled into Mexico from the United States between 2005 and early 2009—but that arsenal amounted to only 17 percent of Mexico's illegal firearms.[35] Others come from various countries in Central and South America.

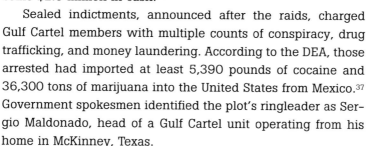

OPERATION PUMA

On August 16, 2007, the DEA and the U.S. Attorney's office for the northern district of Texas announced the completion of "Operation Puma," an investigation launched in early 2005 against Mexico's Gulf Cartel. Collaborating with the U.S. Marshals Service, the Bureau of Immigration and Customs Enforcement, the Texas Department of Public Safety, and local police in 11 Texas cities, DEA agents had served 19 search warrants and arrested 30 suspected drug traffickers. The raiders also seized 609 pounds of cocaine, 900 pounds of marijuana, and some $2.5 million in cash.[36]

Sealed indictments, announced after the raids, charged Gulf Cartel members with multiple counts of conspiracy, drug trafficking, and money laundering. According to the DEA, those arrested had imported at least 5,390 pounds of cocaine and 36,300 tons of marijuana into the United States from Mexico.[37] Government spokesmen identified the plot's ringleader as Sergio Maldonado, head of a Gulf Cartel unit operating from his home in McKinney, Texas.

James Capra, in charge of the DEA's Dallas field office, told reporters:

> This investigation began here in the Dallas Division Office more than two and a half years ago. As the investigation progressed, it became evident that the tentacles

"PLAN MEXICO"

Hoping to end Mexico's bloody drug war *and* curb the flow of illegal drugs to America, Congress authorized $1.6 billion for the three-year Mérida Initiative in 2008. Mexico received $400 million that year, of which $204 million was earmarked for purchase of eight military helicopters and two Cessna surveillance airplanes. Congress also specified that Mexico must spend $73.5 million for judicial reform and improvement of human rights nationwide.[38]

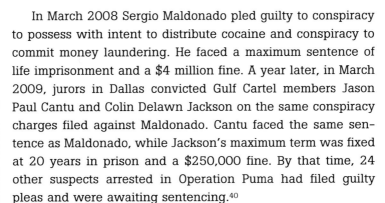

of this drug trafficking enterprise spanned both national and international territories. As criminal members were identified, the scope and magnitude of this organization's destructive powers became apparent. We knew that the mission to dismantle this criminal enterprise would be immense and tedious but one that we could accomplish with fostered law enforcement partnerships both in our own backyard and abroad. Today, we stand shoulder-to-shoulder with our law enforcement partners to announce the successful completion of this investigation. We are proud to have not only dismantled this international drug trafficking organization, but to have erased the stronghold it has had on so many of our communities.[39]

In March 2008 Sergio Maldonado pled guilty to conspiracy to possess with intent to distribute cocaine and conspiracy to commit money laundering. He faced a maximum sentence of life imprisonment and a $4 million fine. A year later, in March 2009, jurors in Dallas convicted Gulf Cartel members Jason Paul Cantu and Colin Delawn Jackson on the same conspiracy charges filed against Maldonado. Cantu faced the same sentence as Maldonado, while Jackson's maximum term was fixed at 20 years in prison and a $250,000 fine. By that time, 24 other suspects arrested in Operation Puma had filed guilty pleas and were awaiting sentencing.[40]

While some critics condemn any federal spending outside the United States, supporters of the Mérida Initiative noted that much of the money would never leave America. All aircraft purchased by Mexico, as well as other surveillance equipment, computers, and law enforcement case-management software, would be sold by firms in the United States. Another $300 million was pledged by Congress for 2009, but budgetary concerns stalled allocations for 2010.[41]

Opponents of the Mérida Initiative call it "Plan Mexico," comparing it to an earlier antidrug program called "Plan Colombia." That program granted Colombian officials $7.5 billion in 2000 for suppression of cocaine trafficking and other uses similar to those of the Mérida Initiative. In 2004 Congress appropriated $727 million more for the Andean Counterdrug Initiative, $463 million of which went to Colombia. And yet, despite early claims that Plan Colombia had reduced cocaine cultivation by 50 percent, an April 2006 statement from the Office of National Drug Control Policy admitted that production of coca *increased* by 26 percent from 2004 to 2005.[42]

However bad things seem in Mexico, DEA spokesmen take an optimistic view. In April 2009 Acting Administrator Michele Leonhart told reporters, "Our view is that the violence we have been seeing is a signpost of the success our very courageous Mexican counterparts are having. The cartels are acting out like caged animals, because they *are* caged animals."[43] Only time will tell if that view is correct.

Cocaine Cowboys

Isla de Coiba, Panama

On March 18, 2007, a U.S. Coast Guard maritime patrol aircraft sighted the *Gatsun,* a ship registered in Panama, sailing north along that country's Pacific coastline. The plane's pilot alerted two Coast Guard cutters, the *Alameda* and the *Hamilton,* assigned to patrol Panamanian waters under a treaty signed by Panama and the United States. The cutters intercepted the *Gatsun* near Panama's Isla de Coiba, where crewmen boarded the ship to search it for illegal drugs. The cargo they discovered—42,845 pounds of cocaine—broke all records for cocaine seizures up to that time.[1]

DEA Administrator Karen Tandy told reporters, "This weekend Mexican drug traffickers were awaiting the arrival of 19 metric tons of cocaine that is now in the hands of U.S. law enforcement instead of the hands of drug traffickers and abusers. This record-breaking seizure denied the Mexican drug lords $300 million in drug revenue. This lost drug revenue, combined with last week's unrelated record-breaking $205 million cash seizure by the Government of Mexico working in partnership with DEA, dealt Mexican traffickers a one-two punch: they're down more than half a billion dollars in blood money in just 48 hours."[2]

The *Gatsun*'s 14 crew members, all Mexican and Panamanian citizens, were held for prosecution on drug-trafficking charges. Prior to capture of the *Gatsun,* the largest maritime cocaine seizures on record included the capture of 30,109 pounds from the stateless vessel *Lina*

Maria on September 17, 2004; 26,397 pounds from the Cambodian-flagged vessel *Svesda Maru* on May 1, 2001; and 26,369 pounds from the Belize-flagged vessel *San Jose* on September 23, 2004.[3]

"SNOW" STORMS

Cocaine is a crystalline tropane alkaloid obtained from leaves of the coca plant, native to the Andes Mountains of South America. Its many modern nicknames include "coke," "snow," "blow," "girl," and "Bolivian marching powder."[4]

Historians date coca's first use by humans, who chewed the raw leaves, to 3000 B.C. The Inca established large coca plantations in the 15th century, which were taken over by Spanish invaders a hundred years later. The new drug proved so popular in Spain that South American landowners were allowed to pay their taxes with coca leaves. Even the church became involved, as the bishop of Cuzco, Peru, claimed 10 percent of the yearly crop.[5]

Cocaine as we know it today was isolated by German chemist Friedrich Gaedcke in 1855. Fifteen years later, wine spiked with cocaine was popular in France. Vassili von Anrep, a chemist at Germany's University of Würzburg, performed the first experiments using cocaine as a medical painkiller in 1879. Psychiatrist Sigmund Freud began using cocaine and touting its medical value in 1884.[6]

Recreational use of cocaine soon surpassed science. In 1885 the U.S. manufacturer Parke-Davis sold cocaine cigarettes, powder, and injectable liquid complete with syringes, promising the drug would "supply the place of food, make the coward brave, the silent eloquent and . . . render the sufferer insensitive to pain." A year later, John Pemberton introduced Coca-Cola, made from syrup laced with cocaine and caffeine. (The cocaine was removed from Coke in 1901.) Popular Sears & Roebuck catalogues, first published in 1888, offered syringes of cocaine for $1.50 each.[7]

PROHIBITION

Cocaine's addictive properties were recognized by 1900, but American officials were not worried at first. In 1903, the *American Journal of Pharmacy* claimed that cocaine users were the dregs of society, "bohemians, gamblers, high- and low-class prostitutes, night porters, bell boys, burglars, racketeers, pimps, and casual laborers."[8]

Shock set in during 1912, when the government recorded 5,000 cocaine-related deaths. Two years later, Dr. Christopher Koch of Pennsylvania's State Pharmacy Board added a racist note, telling Congress, "Most of the attacks upon the white women of the South are the direct result of a cocaine-crazed Negro brain." In December 1914 Congress passed the Harrison Narcotics Tax Act, imposing "a special tax on all persons who produce, import, manufacture, compound, deal in, dispense, sell, distribute, or give away opium or coca leaves, their salts, derivatives, or preparations, and for other purposes."[9]

Even then, cocaine was not officially a controlled substance until October 1970, when it was listed in Schedule II of the Comprehensive Drug Abuse and Control Act. Unlike the drugs listed in Schedule I, cocaine was ranked with those having "a currently accepted medical use in treatment in the United States or a currently accepted medical use with severe restrictions."[10]

The new law recognized cocaine's increasing popularity throughout America, with users found anywhere from urban ghettos to corporate boardrooms and Hollywood studios. Within a decade, cocaine was everywhere, its prevalence noted from plummeting prices. In 1981 a kilogram of pure cocaine cost $55,000; three years later, the same amount cost only $25,000.[11]

CARTEL WARS

As with heroin and other drugs in Mexico, production and smuggling of cocaine fell under the control of large, violent cartels. One of the earliest was Bolivia's Santa Cruz Cartel, also known as "The Corporation," founded in the mid-1970s by wealthy rancher Robert Suárez Gómez (1932–2000). Gómez grew coca and sold its paste to Colombia's Medellín Cartel, amassing a personal fortune exceeding $400 million. In 1983 he offered to pay off Bolivia's foreign debt of $3 billion in return for legal immunity, but the offer was refused. Imprisoned in 1988, Gómez served seven years, then retired from drug trafficking.[12]

The most notorious cocaine cartels were based in Colombia. They include the following organizations:

- The *Cali Cartel*, founded by the Rodríguez Orejuela brothers and José Santacruz-Londoño in the 1960s, known as "Cali's Gentlemen" for their prominent social backgrounds.[13] Starting as a gang of ransom kidnappers, the "gentlemen" switched to drug trafficking in the early 1970s. Ironically, leftist guerrillas kidnapped Santacruz-Londoño's daughter in 1992, demanding a $10 million ransom, but cartel gunmen killed 20 members of the Colombian Communist Party to secure her release.[14] Smuggling became more costly in 1991, when federal agents seized 50 tons of cocaine and $15 million in assets from cartel associates.[15] The Rodríguez brothers were extradited to Miami in 2006 and pled guilty on trafficking charges, forfeiting assets worth $2.1 billion.[16]

- The *Medellín Cartel*, founded by Carlos Lehder-Rivas and George Jung, later dominated by their partner Pablo Escobar. This cartel funneled drugs through the Bahamas to America. It was exposed for the first time in July 1979, when a shootout at Miami's Dadeland

Colombian police fingerprint one of the former bosses of the powerful Cali Cartel, Miguel Rodriguez Orejuela, before he is extradited to the United States. *(Colombian Police/Handout/ Reuters/Corbis)*

Medellín Cartel kingpin Pablo Escobar dominated the global cocaine trade throughout the 1980s. *(AP Photo)*

Mall left two smugglers dead. Ten years later, fear of extradition to America prompted the cartel's leaders to declare "total and absolute war" against Colombia's government, resulting in thousands of murders.[17] That violence sparked harsh reactions, result-

PABLO ESCOBAR (1949–1993)

In 1989 *Forbes* magazine ranked Pablo Escobar Gaviria as the seventh-richest man on Earth, with a personal fortune of $25 billion earned from cocaine trafficking.[18] Ironically, during his early years, he never planned to be a criminal.

Escobar studied political science at Colombia's University of Antioquia, but had to drop out when he could not afford the school's fees. Later, he earned money by recycling headstones from abandoned cemeteries through a shop his uncle owned. Soon Escobar recognized the profits made by others smuggling drugs to the United States and joined the Medellín Cartel, rising swiftly through its ranks thanks to a combination of intelligence and raw brutality.

In 1982 Escobar won election to the lower house of Colombia's Congress, as a member of the Colombian Liberal Party. He already knew—and had bribed—most of the country's leading politicians, but lawmaking was merely one of Escobar's hobbies. Another, construction of numerous churches around Medellín, endeared him to working-class people and peasants, enhancing Escobar's image as a benevolent "Robin Hood" figure.

ing in Escobar's death and the slaying of other cartel members by civilian vigilantes. Today, most of the gang's surviving leaders are in prison.

o The *North Coast Cartel*, led by Alberto "The Snail" Orlandez-Gamboa until his arrest in 1998. This syndicate operated chiefly through the Bahamas, where members of the cartel-allied Arana Nasser family owned 270 separate properties, including the luxurious Hotel El Prado. In December 1998 American and Swiss authorities divided $175 million in cash seized from the North Coast Cartel.[19] Over the next three years, assassination and imprisonment removed most of the cartel's leaders.

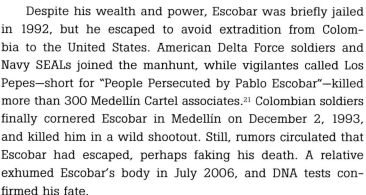

The truth was very different. Controlling an estimated 80 percent of the world's cocaine traffic in the 1980s, Escobar defended his empire with ruthless violence. His motto—*plata o plomo* ("silver or lead," in Spanish)—plainly stated that those who refused his bribes would be killed. Escobar personally executed cartel members who displeased him, and he ordered countless other murders, with victims including three Colombian presidential candidates, an attorney general, a justice minister, dozens of journalists, more than 200 judges, and over 1,000 police officers.[20]

Despite his wealth and power, Escobar was briefly jailed in 1992, but he escaped to avoid extradition from Colombia to the United States. American Delta Force soldiers and Navy SEALs joined the manhunt, while vigilantes called Los Pepes—short for "People Persecuted by Pablo Escobar"—killed more than 300 Medellín Cartel associates.[21] Colombian soldiers finally cornered Escobar in Medellín on December 2, 1993, and killed him in a wild shootout. Still, rumors circulated that Escobar had escaped, perhaps faking his death. A relative exhumed Escobar's body in July 2006, and DNA tests confirmed his fate.

- The *North Valley Cartel,* rising to prominence in the 1990s, as the Cali and Medellín Cartels declined. In May 2004 a racketeering indictment charged nine cartel leaders with smuggling 1.2 million pounds of cocaine into America since 1990, valued in excess of $10 billion. The charges also stated that the gang "used violence and brutality to further its goals, including the murder of rivals, individuals who failed to pay for cocaine, and associates who were believed to be working as informants."[22] Meanwhile, conflict within the cartel claimed more than 1,000 lives during 2003 and 2004.[23] DEA spokesmen describe the cartel as defunct since fugitive leader Diego Montoya Sánchez's arrest in December 2008.

COCAINE WARS

The DEA and other agencies have done their best to halt importation of cocaine to the United States. Between 1986 and 2009, DEA agents seized 3,523,962 pounds of the drug nationwide, excluding other large amounts captured by the Coast Guard, Customs, and state or local police departments.[24] In the 12 months between October 1, 2004, and September 30, 2005, federal courts sentenced 10,838 defendants in cases involving cocaine. Of those, 10,496 were charged with trafficking.[25]

Despite such efforts, large quantities of cocaine still reach American users each year. Proof of the increased supply is seen in falling prices charged for drugs of greater purity. According to the Office of National Drug Control Policy, the street price for one gram of cocaine dropped from $544.59 in 1981 to $106.54 in 2003, while wholesale prices fell from $201.18 per gram to $37.96. During the same period, the purity of confiscated drugs increased from 40 percent to 70 percent.[26]

CRACK ATTACK

In the mid-1980s a new form of cocaine—called "crack" or "rock"—appeared on America's streets. Crack is produced by dissolving powdered cocaine in a mixture of water and ammonia or baking soda, boiling the mixture until solid "rocks" are formed. Relatively cheap and easy to produce, crack is usually smoked and is highly addictive, reportedly hooking some users after two or three doses. First noted in urban ghettos, crack soon spread nationwide. In 1998 alone, an estimated 971,000 Americans smoked crack, of whom 462,000 were white, 324,000 were African American, and 157,000 were Hispanic.[27] By April 2003, the National Drug Intelligence Center reported that 6,222,000 Americans had tried crack at least once in their lives. That number included 150,000 minors aged 12 to 17 and 1,003,000 persons aged 18 to 25.[28]

A controversial series of newspaper articles, published by California's *San Jose Mercury News* in August 1996, charged that the U.S. Central Intelligence Agency (CIA) created America's crack epidemic by selling cocaine to street gangs and using the money to finance illegal guerrilla warfare in Central America.[29] Whatever the truth of those claims, two gangs named in the series certainly dominated crack trafficking from the 1980s onward.

The Crips, founded in Los Angeles during 1971, claimed 35,000 members nationwide by 2002. Initially engaged in robberies and battles for "turf," the Crips turned to widespread drug dealing in the early 1980s, with that traffic and the conflicts it produced resulting in hundreds of murders. A rival gang, the Bloods, was organized in 1972 and presently claims 30,000 active members.[30] By 2009, authorities asserted that drug-related violence between Crips and Bloods had claimed more than 15,000 lives in Los Angeles alone.[31]

NARCO-TERRORISM

While criminal gangs have fought each other throughout history, Colombian cartels raised the ante by declaring war against their nation's government in 1989. Long before that announcement, however, some investigators blamed the Medellín Cartel for financing a leftist attack on Bogotá's Palace of Justice that claimed 120 lives—including 11 of the country's 25 supreme court justices—in November 1985.[32] Other acts of terrorism linked to drug cartels include the following:

- *September 2, 1989*: The car bombing of a Bogotá newspaper office, wounding 84 victims.[33]
- *November 27, 1989*: The bombing of Avianca Flight 203, killing all 110 persons aboard. The intended target, a Colombian presidential candidate, missed the flight.[34]
- *December 6, 1989*: A bombing at the Bogotá headquarters of Colombia's Administrative Department of Security, killing 52 persons, injuring approximately 1,000, and destroying 300 commercial properties.[35]
- *May 13, 1990*: Bombings at two shopping malls, killing 25 and wounding 163.[36]
- *February 16, 1991*: A bomb detonated at Medellín's popular bullfighting ring, killing 22.[37]
- *April 15, 1993*: Another car bomb killed 15 and injured more than 100 at a Bogotá shopping mall.[38]
- Aside from bombings, some observers blame drug cartels for 3,500 murders committed in Medellín during the early 1990s, with victims including 500 police officers.[39]

COCAINE TODAY

DEA spokesmen report that Colombia's huge drug cartels have been smashed, but the traffic continues, much of it carried on by Mexican cartels. Colombia remains the world's leading producer of cocaine, with 167,000 hectares under coca cultivation in 2007, producing 590 tons of pure cocaine yearly. Peru ranks second, producing 232 tons per year, while third-ranked Bolivia refines an average 132 tons of pure cocaine yearly. The United States leads all other nations in cocaine consumption—averaging an estimated 419 tons per year.[40]

Halting that tidal wave of drugs has so far proved impossible, despite large seizures made by the DEA, Coast Guard, and Customs,

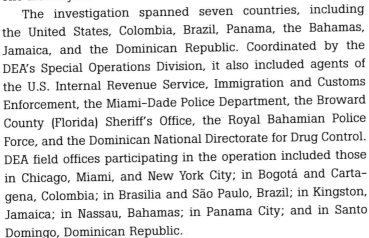

OPERATION CALI EXCHANGE

On December 8, 2005, DEA Administrator Karen Tandy announced the culmination of "Operation Cali Exchange," which targeted Colombian drug traffickers and money launderers. Twenty-four indictments had produced 18 arrests, and raiders seized $7 million in cash, 4,635 pounds of cocaine, 518 pounds of marijuana, three homes, eight cars, one boat, and one motorcycle.[41]

The investigation spanned seven countries, including the United States, Colombia, Brazil, Panama, the Bahamas, Jamaica, and the Dominican Republic. Coordinated by the DEA's Special Operations Division, it also included agents of the U.S. Internal Revenue Service, Immigration and Customs Enforcement, the Miami-Dade Police Department, the Broward County (Florida) Sheriff's Office, the Royal Bahamian Police Force, and the Dominican National Directorate for Drug Control. DEA field offices participating in the operation included those in Chicago, Miami, and New York City; in Bogotá and Cartagena, Colombia; in Brasilia and São Paulo, Brazil; in Kingston, Jamaica; in Nassau, Bahamas; in Panama City; and in Santo Domingo, Dominican Republic.

Operation Cali Exchange was part of the DEA's wider, long-running "Money Trail Initiative," which had recovered $43.6

plus various state and local law enforcement agencies. DEA seizures in recent years include 427 pounds of cocaine intercepted in March 2006; 104,621 pounds in May 2006; 9,512 pounds in February 2007; 42,845 pounds in March 2007; 484 pounds in May 2007; 1,663 pounds in August 2007; 4,800 pounds in September 2008; 38,124 pounds in December 2008; and 26,400 pounds in February 2009.[42]

Even so, a statement issued by the DEA notes:

> The amount of cocaine available in domestic drug markets appears to meet user demand in most markets, without observable shortfall . . . . Control over wholesale cocaine distribution

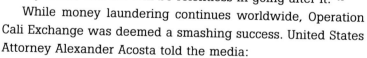

million in drug money since its inception. The program's special target was a network called the Colombian Black Market Peso Exchange, used to launder drug profits through American banks before returning "clean" money to leaders of the Cali Cartel. As DEA Administrator Tandy explained, "Drug traffickers are using their profits to burrow into our neighborhoods and corrupt legitimate banking systems. In major drug trafficking operations, money is the thread that unravels the drugs and devastation otherwise hidden by dealers. DEA knows where money leads, and we will be relentless in going after it."[43]

While money laundering continues worldwide, Operation Cali Exchange was deemed a smashing success. United States Attorney Alexander Acosta told the media:

> This investigation and prosecution strikes at the heart of this international drug organization and is aimed at dismantling the entire drug trafficking organization, from top to bottom. The indictment disrupts every aspect of this drug trafficking network, bringing to justice those responsible for producing the cocaine in South America, those who imported it and sold it in the United States, those who funded and profited from the drug trade, and those who delivered the money back to the drug dealers.[44]

by Mexican criminal groups has been increasing for several years and is likely to continue to increase in the near term. Cocaine transportation data indicate that most cocaine available in U.S. drug markets is smuggled into the country via the U.S.-Mexico border. As Mexican criminal groups control an increasing percentage of the cocaine smuggled into the country, their influence over wholesale distribution will rise even in areas previously controlled by other groups, including areas of the Northeast and Florida/Caribbean Regions."[45]

Within America, the agency reports,

Cocaine is distributed in nearly every large and midsize city; however, analysis of cocaine seizure data indicates that several specific cities serve as national-level cocaine distribution centers through which most domestic cocaine flows. Midlevel and retail-level distribution of the drug in these and most other cities is controlled primarily by organized gangs; however, in smaller cities and rural communities retail distribution typically is controlled by local independent dealers.[46]

The 96-year struggle to rid America of cocaine continues.

Heroin Trails

New York City

On February 1, 2006, DEA spokesmen announced the culmination of "Operation Liquid Heroin," resulting in the arrest of 22 Colombians charged with smuggling 53 pounds of heroin into the United States.[1]

The smuggling ring used various unusual methods of transporting drugs. One technique involved "swallowers," persons who swallow packets of heroin to sneak them past customs inspectors. Another plan used puppies that had packets of liquid heroin surgically implanted in their bodies. The DEA found six puppies carrying nearly seven pounds of heroin. Other shipments concealed heroin in body creams, aerosol cans, and hollow beads.[2]

Agent John Gilbride told reporters, "The organization's outrageous and heinous smuggling method of implanting heroin inside puppies is a true indication of the extent that drug dealers go to make their profit. This investigation identified the individuals who were responsible for overseeing and smuggling millions of dollars worth of heroin from Colombia to the East Coast."[3]

"JOY PLANTS"

Heroin is a synthetic opiate derived from morphine, a natural substance extracted from the seedpods of opium poppies. It appears in various forms, all of which are highly addictive. Common nicknames for heroin include "H," "horse," "junk," "smack," and "scag."[4]

The first discovery of opium was not recorded, but Sumerian farmers cultivated the poppies by 3400 B.C., calling them *hul gil* ("joy plants"). Egypt had large poppy fields by 1300 B.C., and growers sold their crop to Phoenician traders who spread it throughout the Mediterranean and Europe. Greek physician Hippocrates, the "father of medicine," acknowledged opium's medical uses in 460 B.C. Alexander the Great carried opium to India and Persia (now Iran) in 330 B.C.[5]

Use of opium in Europe was taboo during the Inquisition (1184–1241), because church leaders linked it to the Far East and to Satan. Its popularity revived during the 16th century, as European traders grew rich selling opium in China. Swiss physician Paracelsus helped the European trade in 1597, when he began prescribing laudanum—a narcotic consisting of an alcohol solution of opium or any preparation in

Seven plastic packets containing liquid heroin that were surgically removed from live puppies are shown in a DEA photo. The 10 puppies were rescued during a recent raid on a laboratory in Colombia where authorities claim that they were being surgically implanted with packets of liquid heroin and transported to the United States. The packets were discovered in 2005 as a result of a DEA-led initiative called "Operation Liquid Heroin." *(AP Photo/DEA)*

Six of the 10 puppies that were used by Colombian drug traffickers as drug mules are shown in the back of a pick-up truck in Colombia. The 10 puppies were rescued during a raid on a laboratory in Colombia in 2005. *(AP Photo/DEA)*

which opium is the main ingredient—as a painkiller. Chinese Emperor Yongzheng banned opium in 1729, but European traders ignored his decree. By 1750, the British East India Company dominated the opium trade between India and China.[6]

In the 19th century many patent medicines included opium. German pharmacist Friedrich Sertürner discovered morphine in 1803, and physicians called it "God's own medicine," for its reliability in killing pain.[7]

In 1816 American millionaire John Jacob Astor smuggled Turkish opium to China on ships owned by his fur company. French chemist Pierre Robiquet isolated a new painkiller, codeine, from opium in 1832. In 1839 British authorities blamed opium for more accidental poisoning deaths than any other substance—186 cases, including the deaths of 72 children. The following year, 24,000 pounds of opium entered the United States, prompting customs officials to impose a special tax on drug shipments. English chemist C. R. Wright synthesized heroin from morphine in 1874, although the name was not coined until 1895. Ironically, physicians offered heroin as a means of helping morphine addicts break their habit.[8]

HOOKING AMERICA

Historian Edward Brecher describes post–Civil War America as a "dope fiend's paradise," where opiates were "as freely accessible as aspirin is today." Doctors prescribed opiates to their patients, but addicts could find the same products without prescriptions at pharmacies, groceries, and general stores. The state of Iowa alone had 3,000 opiate vendors between 1883 and 1885. One wholesale drug house offered more than 600 patent medicines containing opiates. A survey of 10,000 prescriptions filled by 35 Boston pharmacies in 1888 found that 1,481 included opiates.[9]

Surveys reveal that roughly two-thirds of America's 19th-century opiate addicts were women. The average age of female addicts nationwide was 39 years, while males were slightly older, with an average age of 41. A majority of identified addicts were white, contradicting racist stereotypes of minorities as the most prevalent drug abusers.[10]

Congress noted the problem and responded with a higher tax on opiates in 1890, then banned importation of opium for smoking with the Opium Exclusion Act of 1909. Next came the 1914 Harrison Narcotics Act, mandating registration of physicians who prescribed opiates. In 1922 the Narcotic Import and Export Act restricted traffic in crude opium to supplies intended for medical use. Two years later, the Heroin Act banned importation, manufacture, or possession of heroin, regardless of intended use.[11]

One change resulting from the new laws was a shift in who used heroin. In 1918 the U.S. Treasury Department found that "drug addiction is about equally prevalent in both sexes." That ratio kept changing, until male addicts in the 1960s outnumbered female heroin users five to one. By the 1970s, 86 percent of identified opiate addicts were 30 years old or younger, and nearly half were African American.[12]

STRANGE BEDFELLOWS

New restrictions shifted control of the opium/heroin market from governments to criminal cartels, but some government agencies were still involved in drug trafficking. World War II disrupted the international traffic and America's Opium Poppy Control Act of 1942 banned unlicensed cultivation, but the trade survived, waiting to blossom once again in peacetime.[13]

American officials deported Mafia boss Charles Luciano to Italy in 1946, but he soon surfaced in Cuba, helping former Prohibition-era bootleggers expand the world heroin trade. Corsican gangsters refined Turkish opium in France, in partnership with the U.S. Central Intelligence Agency (CIA). The mobsters harassed French communists, and in return the CIA protected drug routes to America. Corrupt officials took their share of the profits, until Turkey banned opium cultivation in 1972 and the U.S. Bureau of Narcotics and Dangerous Drugs joined local police to arrest smugglers and dealers on American soil.[14]

Meanwhile, the pattern was repeated in Southeast Asia. Burma (now Myanmar) won independence from Britain in January 1948, and quickly expanded its opium crop. Plantations in French Indochina created a "Golden Triangle" of opium production, providing addicts worldwide with heroin called "China White." Burma outlawed opium in 1962, but production continued under drug lords like Khun Sa, while the escalating war in Vietnam witnessed renewal of the CIA's outlaw alliance with heroin smugglers.[15]

In the early 1960s the Federal Bureau of Narcotics seized 200 pounds of heroin per year, while smugglers imported 5,000 pounds yearly. Corsican traffickers supplied 80 to 90 percent of those drugs until authorities cracked the "French Connection," then the balance shifted toward Asia. By 1970, an estimated 750,000 Americans were heroin addicts. That fact prompted passage of the 1970 Comprehensive Drug Abuse and Control Act, listing heroin among controlled substances having "no currently accepted medical use in treatment in the United States."[16]

GLOBAL SMACKDOWN

By 1973, heroin was being smuggled into the United States from several regions. Southeast Asia's Golden Triangle competed with Central Asia's "Golden Crescent" and several countries in Latin America.

The Golden Crescent overlaps three nations—Afghanistan, Iran, and Pakistan—where, once again, America's foreign policy influenced

KHUN SA (1933–2007)

Asia's "Opium King" was born Chang Chi-fu. At age 16, after Mao Zedong's communists won control of China, he took the name Khun Sa ("Prince Prosperous") and joined the Kuomintang—the Chinese nationalist party led by Chiang Kai-shek. While Chiang led most of his followers to Taiwan, Khun Sa remained in Burma to form his own anti-communist army, financed with opium and heroin.

Khun Sa's politics were often confusing. He helped Burmese authorities hunt rebels, but also battled with government troops. He supported the Kuomintang at times, and then fought against its soldiers. Burmese authorities arrested Khun Sa in 1969, but he was freed in 1973, after his soldiers kidnapped two Russian doctors. Moving his headquarters to Thailand in 1976, Khun Sa joined revolutionaries who opposed both the Thai and Burmese governments—but warfare never distracted him from drug trafficking.

In 1989 New York prosecutors indicted Khun Sa for smuggling 1,000 tons of heroin into America. Khun Sa countered by asking the U.S. government to buy his drugs, and thus avert their sale to international dealers. "If you buy the heroin," he said, "I can stop the trade and make the farmers cultivate something else."[17] Washington responded by posting a $2 million reward for his capture.

Khun Sa surrendered to Burmese police in January 1996, but they refused to extradite him for trial in America. *The Times* of London reported that Khun Sa had struck a deal, retiring from the drug trade to manage public buses and real estate in Rangoon. DEA spokesmen called Khun Sa "a ruthless criminal who is probably the largest heroin-trafficker in the world," to which he replied: "Today's friend could be tomorrow's enemy. Today's enemy could be tomorrow's friend. When the DEA gives the Thais money they come and attack me. When I give them money, they go away again."[18]

Diabetes claimed Khun Sa's life on October 26, 2007, at age 74.

heroin trafficking. Russian troops occupied Afghanistan from December 1979 to February 1989, resisted by guerrillas known as *mujahideen*, whose ranks included future terrorist Osama bin Laden. Between 1980 and 1990, the CIA gave the mujahideen more than $2 billion in cash and weapons, knowing that the guerrillas also smuggled opium and heroin. In 1983 mujahideen produced 4.5 tons of heroin that made its way into the United States. Five years later they produced 880 tons.[19]

Meanwhile, Mexico and Colombia claimed their share of the market as police focused on the Golden Triangle and Golden Crescent. Mexico's black tar heroin is cheaply produced and easily smuggled over the same border crossed by 11 million illegal immigrants yearly.[20] Mexican authorities cooperated with the United States in 1978, spraying opium crops with the defoliant Agent Orange, but cultivation continued. By 2007, Mexico dominated heroin trafficking in the western United States, with 55 tons imported that year.[21]

Colombia's cartels expanded from cocaine to heroin in the early 1990s, smuggling an estimated four tons of heroin into America during 1991. In January 1992 Bruce Carnes, a spokesman for the ONDCP, told reporters, "Obviously, the Colombian heroin is ominous. They're extremely proficient at their trade." Rensselaer Lee, speaking for Philadelphia's Foreign Policy Research Institute, called the new traffic "a sickening development, one of the worst things that's happened on the drug front in recent years."[22]

In 1988 General Saw Maung overthrew Burma's government and established a new State Law and Order Restoration Council—which, despite its name, increased production of opium and heroin for export. By 1995, the Golden Triangle dominated the global heroin trade, shipping 2,500 tons per year, but 1996 found China, Nigeria, and Colombia "aggressively marketing heroin in the United States and Europe."[23]

Then came 9/11 and the "War on Terror." Once again, everything changed.

NEW WORLD DISORDER

American troops invaded Afghanistan in October 2001, seeking to capture Osama bin Laden and his forces, while dismantling the Taliban regime that supported them. That struggle continues in 2010, but some dramatic changes have occurred in Afghanistan.

Under Taliban rule, Afghanistan's largest opium crop produced 5,060 tons in 1999.[24] In July 2000, Mullah Mohammad Omar banned opium growing and launched an effective drug-eradication program, reducing the amount of land under opium cultivation by 91 percent. In Helmand Province, which produced more than half of Afghanistan's opium, no poppies were grown during 2001.[25]

That picture changed under American occupation. Former CIA-mujahideen supporter Hamid Karzai became president in 2004, and opium production soon surpassed pre-Taliban levels, while some farmers complained that "government officials take bribes for turning a blind eye to the drug trade while punishing poor opium growers."[26] By 2007, 93 percent of all opiates sold worldwide originated from Afghanistan, valued around $4 billion.[27]

Afghanistan remains the world's largest opium/heroin producer in 2010. Although the CIA reported a 22 percent decrease in opium cultivation for 2008, it noted that production "remains at a historically high level," with an estimated 6,050 tons of raw opium and 713 tons of pure heroin. Myanmar placed second in 2008, with 374 tons of opium, a 26 percent increase from 2007.[28] In 2005, the last year with estimates available, Interpol reported that Mexico exported 76 tons of heroin, while Colombia shipped 31 tons.[29]

HORSE TRAILS

Heroin smugglers follow various routes well known to the DEA, trusting bribery, violence, and luck to protect their shipments. Most drugs produced in the Golden Triangle passed through Hong Kong and Bangkok, Thailand, during the 1990s, when traffickers sought new routes in the face of increasing surveillance. Today, many shipments travel down the Mekong River, or overland through Thailand to Malaysia. Chinese Triad syndicates dominate the Southeast Asian traffic, including delivery and distribution in Australia and Canada.[30]

Heroin from the Golden Crescent normally follows one of two paths, known as the Balkan Route and the Silk Route. The Balkan Route is based in Turkey and has three sub-routes. Its northern route passes through Bulgaria and Romania to Austria, Hungary, the Czech Republic, Poland, or Germany. Its central route runs through Bulgaria,

THE PIZZA CONNECTION

The so-called Pizza Connection was a drug network run by members of the Mafia. The network imported heroin to the United States and sold it from various pizza parlors. Established in 1975, with headquarters in Queens, New York, the syndicate smuggled drugs valued at a total of $1.6 billion before authorities cracked down on it in 1984.[31]

Trouble began for the smugglers in Sicily, when customs officers intercepted a shipment of undeclared cash wrapped in pizza aprons. Those arrested were all linked to restaurants in the United States. Prosecutors soon indicted 32 defendants—24 of them in the United States, eight others scattered from Europe to South America. Prior to trial in 1985, one defendant was murdered and another died from natural causes, leaving 22 to face a federal jury.[32]

They included ringleader Gaetano Badalamenti, former boss of the Sicilian Mafia, with various mobsters from both sides of the Atlantic Ocean. One, Gaetano Mazzara, was murdered during the trial—which proved to be one of the longest in New York history, lasting from October 1985 to March 1987. At its conclusion, two defendants were acquitted and 19 were convicted on multiple counts of drug trafficking and racketeering. Badalamenti received a 45-year sentence and died in prison seven years later. Others were sentenced to prison terms ranging from five to 45 years. One of those acquitted, Badalamenti's nephew Vito, is presently on Italy's list of "30 Most Wanted" Mafia fugitives.[33]

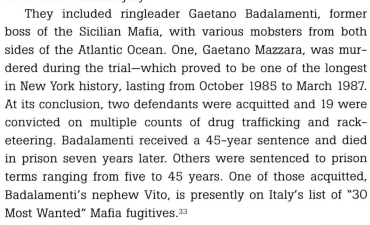

the former Yugoslav Republic of Macedonia, Serbia, Montenegro, Bosnia and Herzegovina, Croatia, and Slovenia, into Italy and Austria. The southern route passes through Greece and Albania to Italy.[34]

The Silk Route crosses Central Asia, with 40 percent of Afghanistan's heroin and morphine passing through Iran, despite significant seizures made there. The CIA's report on Iranian drug trafficking notes that the country "remains one of the primary transshipment routes for Southwest Asian heroin to Europe; suffers one of the highest opiate addiction rates in the world, and has an increasing problem with synthetic drugs; lacks anti-money laundering laws."[35]

In recent years, African addicts have consumed increasing amounts of heroin from the Golden Crescent. Interpol reports that drugs are smuggled into Africa by air, by sea, and overland in both commercial and passenger vehicles. Nigerian gangs dominate the traffic in West Africa and Ethiopia is the primary transit hub for illegal drugs in East Africa.[36]

Mexican drug cartels have relatively free access to the United States, and they presently dominate heroin traffic west of the Mississippi River. Colombian smugglers use various routes passing through Mexico, Argentina, Costa Rica, Ecuador, Guatemala, Panama, and Venezuela. Their greatest influence is felt in the eastern United States.[37]

Availability of illegal drugs is judged by their price and purity: High prices and low purity indicate a small supply spread thin, with high demand. Heroin is also ranked by numbers: "No. 1" is morphine base extracted from raw opium; "No. 2" is heroin base derived from morphine; "No. 3" is 20 to 30 percent pure heroin, normally smoked; and "No. 4" is 80 to 90 percent pure, typically injected.[38]

In 2004 a kilogram of Pakistani No. 3 heroin cost $2,250, while a kilogram of No. 4 cost $4,076. In Afghanistan the same drugs sold for $1,600 and $4,000 per kilogram, respectively. In Colombia, a kilogram of No. 4 cost $10,149 wholesale in 2004, while the same package sold in the United States for $66,250.[39]

An indication of America's available supply is seen in falling prices. According to the ONDCP, the street price for one gram of heroin fell from $1,974.49 in 1981 to $361.95 in 2003. Wholesale prices dropped, during that same period, from $1,007.60 per gram to $139.22. And while prices plummeted, purity increased. At the retail level, heroin "improved" from 11 percent pure in 1981 to 32 percent in 2003. The wholesale product rose from 12 percent pure to 46 percent.[40]

SMACK NATION

America remains the world's largest consumer of heroin, despite the best efforts of DEA agents and other law enforcement agencies.[41]

A DEA agent announces the details of arrests made in connection
with 15 to 17 kilograms of heroin shipped from Colombia to Miami
inside tractor chains during a news conference in Miami in January
2006. *(AP Photo/Lynne Sladky)*

Between 1986 and 2006, the DEA seized 31,719 pounds of heroin nationwide.[42] More recent seizures include 11 pounds in February 2007, 550 pounds in March 2007, 770 pounds in May 2007, 19 pounds in September 2008, another 19 pounds in December 2008, and 18 pounds in February 2009.[43]

While no one defends heroin addiction as a desirable lifestyle, confusion surrounds its actual danger. The Schaffer Library of Drug Policy pegs America's yearly heroin death toll at an average 400 lives.[44] Virginia's Department of Health logged 127 heroin-related deaths statewide between 2004 and 2006.[45] Oregon authorities counted 115 deaths statewide in 2007.[46] New York's Nassau County reported 46 heroin deaths in 2008, with 38 more in 2009.[47]

Despite those figures, some physicians minimize the risk of using heroin. Dr. Andrew Byrne, an Australian specialist in drug addiction treatment, writes, "Unlike alcohol or tobacco, heroin causes no ongoing toxicity to the tissues or organs of the body. Apart from causing some constipation, it appears to have no side effects in most who take it. When administered safely, its use may be consistent with a long and productive life. The principal harm comes from the risk of overdose, problems with injecting, drug impurities, and adverse legal or financial consequences."[48]

American psychiatrist Dr. Stanton Peele agrees. He says: "People rarely die from heroin overdoses—meaning pure concentrations of the drug which simply overwhelm the body's responses. If it is not pure drugs that kill, but impure drugs and the mixture of drugs, then the myth of the heroin overdose can be dangerous. If users had a guaranteed pure supply of heroin which they relied on, there would be little more likelihood of toxic doses than occur with narcotics administered in a hospital."[49] However, providing a pure supply of heroin to accommodate heroin addicts is not a viable policy option.

Crystal
Death

Bethlehem, Pennsylvania

John Acerra was a respected figure in his community. He had joined the Bethlehem Area School District as an elementary school teacher in 1979, rising through its ranks to serve as principal of the Nitschmann Middle School. He seemed to be above reproach until February 28, 2007, when undercover DEA agents arrested him in a sting operation. Federal prosecutors charged Acerra with nine criminal counts, including charges of possession with intent to deliver methamphetamine, delivery of methamphetamine, possession of a controlled substance, and possession with intent to use drug paraphernalia. Acerra was held in lieu of $200,000 bail.[1]

DEA Agent James Kasson told reporters:

Acerra was entrusted with the safety and welfare of young children. Acerra violated that public trust, not only by distributing methamphetamine, but also utilizing the Nitschmann Middle School as a point of distribution. Acerra's arrest defused a potentially harmful and damaging situation where school age children were brought into contact with methamphetamine users, distributors and sources of supply on school grounds.[2]

In August 2007 Acerra pled guilty on two counts of delivering methamphetamine and one count of intent to deliver. He received a prison

HELL ON WHEELS

"Outlaw" motorcycle gangs dominated illegal methamphetamine production in America during the 1980s and early 1990s, before Mexican drug cartels streamlined mass-production. Today, bikers serve more often as distributors in the United States and Canada, buying their supplies from Mexico.[3] The "Big Four" biker gangs include the following:

★ The *Outlaws,* founded in Illinois in 1935, presently claim 200 chapters in the United States, Canada, Europe, Australia, and Asia.[4] Rapid expansion after 1950 paralleled growth of the Hells Angels gang, whose members are bitter enemies of the Outlaws. War between the gangs has claimed hundreds of lives, and the "ADIOS" patch worn by many Outlaws reportedly translates as "*Angels Die in Outlaw States.*" The gang's motto since 1969 is "God Forgives, Outlaws Don't." In 1977 the Outlaws absorbed Canada's largest biker gang, Satan's Choice.[5]

★ The *Hells Angels,* organized in 1947, presently claim 190 chapters in 31 countries worldwide.[6] Many Hells Angels are currently in prison, and many more have been killed by rival

term of two to four years and was released in May 2009, with parole extended to February 2011.[7]

THE NEW "ICE" AGE

Amphetamine and methamphetamine are highly addictive psycho-stimulant drugs that trigger release of the chemicals dopamine, norepinephrine, and serotonin, producing extreme euphoria that commonly results in hyperactivity, hypersexuality, and obsession with a particular task. Anxiety, loss of appetite, and sleep deprivation are common side effects, with many users also taking sedatives to offset these symptoms. Common street names for these drugs include "meth," "ice," "speed," "crystal," "chalk," and "crank."[8]

gangs or enforcers within their own organization. A typical police operation, called "Project E-Pandora," jailed 45 Canadian Hells Angels in 2005, while police seized 792 pounds of illegal drugs, plus numerous weapons and $200,000 in cash.[9]

★ The *Pagans,* founded in 1959, have an estimated 400 members in 11 U.S. states. A national team of 13 "regulators" suppresses dissension within the gang and targets rivals with violence. Crimes commonly associated with the Pagans include drug trafficking, illegal weapons sales, auto theft, arson, and extortion. Authorities report that the gang has close ties to New Jersey's dominant Mafia "family."[10]

★ The *Bandidos,* created in 1966, presently claim 210 chapters in 16 countries worldwide.[11] A Scandinavian drug war between the Bandidos and Hells Angels claimed 11 lives and left 96 persons wounded between 1994 and 1997.[12] An Australian shootout between Bandidos and rival Comancheros killed seven victims in 1984. More recently, in April 2006, Bandidos were charged with killing six of their own members in Canada.[13]

Romanian chemist Lazar Edeleanu first synthesized amphetamine in 1887, calling it phenylisopropylamine, but his discovery inspired no widespread interest. Japanese chemist Nagayoshi Nagai synthesized methamphetamine in 1893, but another Japanese chemist—Akira Ogata—commonly gets credit for creating the drug's crystallized form in 1919. By 1932, amphetamine was available in patent medicines, dubbed Benzedrine. Five years later, the American Medical Association approved its use for treating hyperactivity and narcolepsy. During World War II, both drugs were widely distributed to soldiers on both sides. The U.S. government also dispensed amphetamine to troops in the Korean War of 1950–1953.[14]

Japan was the first nation to suffer a meth addiction epidemic, with 2 million addicts identified nationwide in 1954. Nine years later, California's attorney general requested a ban on injectable ampoules sold in pharmacies without prescriptions. In July 1965 Congress passed the Drug Abuse Control Amendment to the Food, Drug, and Cosmetic Act of 1938, banning unregistered possession, manufacture, or sale of amphetamines or any other drugs with "a potential for abuse because of its depressant or stimulant effect on the central nervous system or its hallucinogenic effect." Five years later, the Comprehensive Drug Abuse Prevention and Control Act placed injectable methamphetamine in Schedule II (listing drugs with "a currently accepted medical use"), while other forms were placed in Schedule III (drugs with "a potential for abuse less than the drugs or other substances in Schedules I and II").[15]

That judgment seemed unrealistic by the 1990s, as methamphetamine became America's third most common drug of choice among abusers (after alcohol and marijuana).[16] In 1996 Congress passed the Methamphetamine Control Act, establishing new controls over key ingredients used to manufacture methamphetamine and increasing penalties for possession, manufacturing, and distribution. More recently, the Combat Methamphetamine Epidemic Act of 2005, signed into law in March 2006, regulates over-the-counter sales of patent medicines containing the precursor chemicals ephedrine, phenylpropanolamine, and pseudoephedrine. Under the new law, no individual may purchase more than 9 grams of any such medicine within a 30-day period.[17]

CRACKING "ICE"

The DEA has energetically pursued meth smugglers, manufacturers, and dealers, both domestically and worldwide. Between 1986 and 2009, DEA agents seized 57,256 pounds of methamphetamine in the United States, a figure that does not include seizures by other federal, state, and local law enforcement agencies.[18] Between 1999 and 2008, the agency also logged 113,464 "meth clandestine laboratory incidents," including raids on illegal labs and discoveries of chemical dump sites.[19] Some of the DEA's more famous anti-meth campaigns include the following:

- *Operation Meta* concluded in December 1997 with 121 arrests, plus seizure of 133 pounds of methamphetamine, 2,420 pounds of cocaine, and 1,765 pounds of marijuana. The operation's target was

A DEA agent shows some of the 187-plus pounds of methamphetamine that was seized at a house in Gwinnett County, Georgia, at a news conference in August 2006. *(AP Photo/Ric Feld)*

a Mexican cartel led by brothers José and Luis Amezcua-Contreras, based in Guadalajara. José Amezcua-Contreras was already in custody, jailed by Mexican authorities in November 1997. Federal officers captured his brother in Guadalajara on June 1, 1998.[20] Mexican authorities dismissed most of the charges in 1998 and refused to extradite the brothers.

- *Operation Mountain Express* culminated in August 2000 with 140 arrests, plus seizures of 22,000 pounds of pseudoephedrine tablets (capable of producing approximately 18,000 pounds of methamphetamine), 83 pounds of finished methamphetamine, two pseudoephedrine extraction laboratories, one methamphetamine laboratory, 136 pounds of chemical solvents and reagents, and $8 million in cash. Raids were conducted in 10 states, spanning the continent from California to New York and Florida.[21]

o *Operation Triple X* concluded in October 2001, when DEA agents in Escondido, California, dismantled an illegal lab manufacturing methamphetamine and MDMA (ecstasy). The campaign drew its name from the "XXX" logo imprinted on the lab's ecstasy tablets. Seized in the raid were 48,000 MDMA tablets, 106 pounds of 3,4-propene (enough to make 500,000 ecstasy tablets), 700 pounds of camphor oil (enough for 1 million ecstasy tablets), 45 gallons of gamma-butyrolactone (used to make the the the "date-rape drug" Gamma-Hydroxybutyric acid, or GHB), one pound of methamphetamine, 15 guns, and $429,000 in cash.[22]

o *Operation Mountain Express III* came to a head in January 2002 with more than 300 arrests, plus seizures including 30 tons of pseudoephedrine, 181 pounds of methamphetamine, nine illegal laboratories, 96 automobiles, several bank accounts, and $16 million in cash. The drug ring purchased its precursor chemicals in Canada and processed them in clandestine labs in 10 U.S. cities, including Chicago, Detroit, Los Angeles, and Phoenix. Materials and finished drugs were transported in vans bearing counterfeit Federal Express logos to divert suspicion.[23]

o *Mantubhai Patel*, production manager and board member of Neil Laboratories in East Windsor, New Jersey, was arrested in January 2002. Neil Laboratories is a legitimate manufacturer and exporter of chemicals and pharmaceuticals, founded in 1993 by Bharat Patel. Mantubhai Patel used his executive position to divert controlled substances from medical use and sell them to drug traffickers across the United States. Prior to Patel's arrest, Neil's headquarters received numerous official warnings based on 50 law enforcement actions in 11 states, which identified 3.5 million illegally diverted pseudoephedrine tablets between February 1999 and April 2001. A federal suspension order accompanied Patel's arrest, barring Neil Laboratories from producing any products containing ephedrine or pseudoephedrine until a court hearing was held.[24]

o *Operation Northern Star,* a joint campaign conducted by the DEA and the Royal Canadian Mounted Police, culminated in April 2003 with 65 arrests in 10 cities, plus seizure of 108 million pseudo-ephedrine tablets destined for illegal labs, where they would have produced 9,000 pounds of methamphetamine valued at $144 million. The tablets came from three Canadian manufacturers—G.C. Medical Products, Formulex, and Frega, Inc.—which were the operation's primary targets. Aside from six corporate executives, those arrested included transporters, manufacturers, distributors, and money launderers active in Chicago; Cincinnati; Detroit; Gulfport, Mississippi; Los Angeles; Montreal, Québec; New York City; Ottawa, Ontario; Riverside, California; and Vancouver, British Colombia.[25]

o Raids in Yuma, Arizona, in December 2004 jailed eight members of a methamphetamine trafficking ring, while seizing 9 pounds of methamphetamine, 1 pound of cocaine, 100 pounds of marijuana, drug packaging materials, five guns, one truck, and $6,000 in cash. DEA spokesmen estimated that the gang had earned $4.8 million per year distributing methamphetamine in Arizona and Southern California. Arizona Attorney General Terry Goddard told reporters, "As these arrests and seizures demonstrate, Arizona has a serious methamphetamine problem. In addition to prosecuting the people involved in this drug ring, I will be going to the legislature with a proposal to help fight the growing meth crisis in Arizona."[26]

o *Operation Global Warming* concluded in March 2005 with 16 arrests, plus seizures including 86 pounds of methamphetamine, 6 pounds of heroin, 1 pound of marijuana, four vehicles, 19 guns, and $209,000 in cash. The traffickers in this case transported illegal drugs from Mexico to Oregon and Washington, traveling along Interstate Highway 5 through California.[27]

o *Operation Three Hour Tour* dismantled three major drug trafficking organizations with international ties and 27 U.S. distribution groups in August 2005. The major drug rings, based in Mexico and Colombia, reportedly served 22,700 American addicts, importing an average 50 pounds of methamphetamine, 20 to 30 pounds of heroin, and 4,000 pounds of cocaine per month. The campaign produced 164 arrests, with seizures including 55 pounds of methamphetamine, 3,163 pounds of powder cocaine, 9.5 ounces of crack cocaine, 15 pounds of heroin, 216 pounds of marijuana, 10,000 doses of Ecstasy, 58 vehicles, 52 guns, and $5.5 million in cash.[28]

o *Operation Wildfire* targeted methamphetamine producers and dealers in 200 American cities from coast to coast. DEA Mobile Enforcement Teams joined state and local police in the August 2005 crackdown, which resulted in 427 arrests. Raiders also seized 209 pounds of methamphetamine, 224,860 tablets of ephedrine, 201,035 tablets of pseudoephedrine, 348 pounds of pseudoephedrine powder, 56 clandestine meth labs, 123 weapons, and 28 vehicles. Thirty endangered children also were removed from homes where drugs were manufactured, packaged, and sold. U.S. Attorney General Alberto Gonzales told reporters, "The Department of Justice is committed to using every available resource to ensure that our streets and neighborhoods are safe and that the methamphetamine problem is brought to an end."[29]

o *Operation Red Dragon* led to the arrest of a Scottish couple, Brian Howes and Kerry Ann Shanks, in January 2007. The Central Scotland Police arrested Howes and Shanks after a federal grand jury in Arizona indicted them on 82 criminal counts. A DEA investigation revealed that the defendants had supplied Arizona meth labs with iodine crystals and red phosphorus, two chemicals essential for conversion of pseudoephedrine into methamphetamine. Two other suspects were jailed in Arizona, one of them employed as a vocational teacher with the Arizona Department of Juvenile Corrections. Transacting business on the Internet, Howes and Shanks sold 319,100 grams of red phosphorus and 45,950 grams of iodine to American customers between August 2004 and November 2006— enough to produce 1,400 pounds of methamphetamine valued at $12.6 million. They also dealt with outlaw labs in Europe, Australia, and New Zealand, among other locations.[30]

o *Operation GhostRider* targeted the Kelly Park Crips and other drug-trafficking gangs active in the vicinity of Pueblo, Colorado. The campaign closed in May 2007 with 28 arrests. DEA agents and local officers also seized 346 grams of methamphetamine, 235 grams of crack cocaine, 11 pounds of powder cocaine, eight guns, four vehicles valued at $35,000, and one bulletproof vest. Alleged ringleader James Bachicha and his associates were indicted under a state law, the Colorado Organized Crime Control Act, but DEA agents joined in the investigation since possession and sale of the various drugs are also federal crimes.[31]

o *Operation Latitude Adjustment* targeted a Mexican drug cartel that smuggled methamphetamine, cocaine, heroin, and marijuana to Atlanta for distribution throughout Alabama, California, Florida, Georgia, New York, North and South Carolina, Tennessee, and Virginia. A federal grand jury indicted 22 defendants on December 4, 2007, and 12 of those were arrested in raids conducted one week later. The California portion of the operation led to the seizure of 604 pounds of methamphetamine, 1,246 pounds of cocaine, 2

Wearing protective masks, DEA agents inspect chemicals used to create methamphetamine. The chemicals were discovered in a makeshift meth lab by St. Louis, Missouri, firefighters. *(Bill Greenblatt/Corbis Sygma)*

pounds of heroin, and over $9 million in cash. In Atlanta over 585 pounds of cocaine were seized along with over $1 million.[32]

○ A record methamphetamine seizure in New Jersey was announced on December 1, 2008. Defendant Alberto Olguin, a Texas resident, was stopped by DEA agents and Passaic County sheriff's

OPERATION PILL CRUSHER

On June 1, 2007, Agent John McBride of the DEA's office in New York City announced the completion of "Operation Pill Crusher," an investigation of persons who violated the Combat Methamphetamine Epidemic Act by purchasing illegal quantities of ephedrine and pseudoephedrine to produce methamphetamine. Ten suspects were arrested in the sweep.[33]

Federal law restricts any individual's purchase of ephedrine or pseudoephedrine to 9 grams within 30 days. The 10 defendants charged in Operation Pill Crusher visited numerous pharmacies in New York and Pennsylvania, collecting much larger amounts, then crushed and processed the tablets to extract the desired chemicals for use in meth labs. Their arrests resulted from collaboration of the DEA, the New York and Pennsylvania State Police, four county sheriffs' offices, and two city police departments.[34]

At the June press conference, U.S. Attorney Glenn Suddaby told reporters:

> Our efforts to reduce the demand for, and supply of, methamphetamine has [sic] special priority. The enactment of retail controls on the sale and purchase of key methamphetamine precursors such as psuedoephedrine and ephedrine should reduce the amount of products readily available that could be used to manufacture methamphetamine. The illicit manufacture of methamphetamine has been the subject of wide-scale national attention in recent years and has been particularly prominent in the Southern Tier area of New York State.[35]

deputies while driving a truck filled with farm produce through West Paterson, New Jersey. Inside the truck, agents found 165 pounds of crystal methamphetamine, with an approximate street value of $11 million. Olguin was held in lieu of $5 million bail, on charges carrying a maximum penalty of 20 years imprisonment. DEA spokesmen credited the bust to diligent investigation by a multiagency task force, but revealed no further details.[36]

DEA spokesmen contend that they are winning the war on methamphetamine. As evidence, they cite reports that the average price for one gram of pure methamphetamine increased by 73 percent—from $141.42 to $244.53—between January and November 2007.[37] Other agency statistics indicate that methamphetamine seizures also increased by 30 percent between 2007 and 2008, from 2,389 pounds to 3,389 pounds.[38] American meth lab "incidents" also increased by 23 percent during the same period, from 5,910 in 2007 to 6,783 in 2008.[39] Clearly, the war is far from over.

Blood Money

Phoenix, Arizona

William Wallace Keegan hated the idea of serving time in prison. After an arrest for marijuana trafficking in 1977, he changed his name to Richard Alan King and endured painful surgery to remove all 10 of his fingerprints. He refused to stop dealing drugs, but did switch from pot to cocaine, in pursuit of higher profits.

The new name dodge protected Keegan for 31 years. He ran cocaine distribution networks from San Diego, California, and Palm Harbor, Florida, but he finally ran out of luck in Phoenix, Arizona, where DEA agents arrested him in January 2008. They had evidence proving that "King" shipped at least 330 pounds of cocaine from Arizona to New York between November 2005 and the date of his arrest—but who was he, exactly?[1]

As it turned out, Keegan's surgeon had not done enough. Modern fingerprint records show the full length of a suspect's fingers, and DEA experts matched Keegan's prints from his 1977 arrest despite the smooth tips. On June 19, 2009, a Phoenix jury convicted Keegan on four counts of possession with intent to distribute cocaine, one count of conspiracy to distribute, and one count of conspiracy to commit money laundering. Each of the drug counts carried a maximum sentence of life imprisonment and a $4 million fine. The money-laundering charge carried a maximum sentence of 20 years and a $500,000 fine.[2]

CLEANING DIRTY MONEY

Money laundering involves the concealment (or "cleaning") of income derived from illegal activity for the purpose of hiding a felon's source of revenue and permit tax payments, thus avoiding prosecution for the separate crime of tax evasion. Eighty-two of the world's 203 countries have laws to punish money laundering; some countries rarely enforce them, while others welcome criminals and their cash.[3]

Organized money laundering in the United States dates from the early 1930s, when federal prosecutors imprisoned several notorious bootleggers for income tax evasion. The Swiss Banking Act of 1934 permitted criminals to hide their loot in numbered bank accounts, and other countries later followed Switzerland's example. Still, criminals wishing to spend money openly in America need some apparently legitimate source to account for the cash.

In 1970 Congress passed the Currency and Foreign Transactions Reporting Act, also known as the Bank Secrecy Act, which requires U.S. financial institutions to report cash transactions exceeding $10,000 to the Internal Revenue Service (IRS). Later federal laws include the Money Laundering Control Act of 1986 and the Money Laundering Suppression Act of 1994. By 2000, more than 170 crimes were listed in U.S. money-laundering statutes, including drug trafficking, fraud, murder for hire, and acts of terrorism.[4] Further provisions were added after the terrorist attacks of September 2001, with the creation of a new Terrorist Finance Tracking Program.

Basic money laundering involves three steps. The first, placement, occurs when criminals insert illegal cash into a legitimate bank or other commercial institution. In the second phase, layering, cash is shuffled through various accounts, which makes the money difficult to follow. In the last step, integration, laundered money re-enters the legitimate economy, typically through business investments or the purchase of high-ticket luxury items.[5] Some specific money-laundering methods include the following:

- "*Cashing up*" is when money is channeled through the bank accounts of legitimate businesses with high cash volumes, such as convenience stores, bars and liquor stores, pawn shops, and gambling casinos, thereby hiding dirty money with the clean. In the case of casinos, rigged winnings may also serve as a source of declarable income.

- *Captive businesses* are specifically created by criminals to receive illicit cash, bank it, and falsely declare it as legitimate taxable income. Also known as "shell" companies, these firms are easily created, and as easily dissolved if the hidden owners suspect they are under investigation.
- Money launderers *structure deposits* to avoid the reporting provisions of U.S. federal statutes. In this system, deposits smaller than

BCCI

Criminals often use legitimate banks to launder their cash, but one bank was created with illegal business in mind. Pakistani financier Agha Hasan Abedi in 1972 founded the Bank of Credit and Commerce International (BCCI), registered in Luxembourg. At its peak, the BCCI had 400 branches in 78 countries; it was ranked as the world's seventh largest bank, with assets exceeding $20 billion.[6]

Nineteen years passed before the bank's criminal activities were exposed. Regulators in America and Britain found the BCCI to be involved in money laundering, bribery, tax evasion, terrorism, arms trafficking, smuggling, illegal immigration, and sale of nuclear technologies. Aside from those crimes, $13 billion of the bank's assets were missing. Investigators declared that the BCCI had been "set up deliberately to avoid centralized regulatory review, and operated extensively in bank secrecy jurisdictions. Its affairs were extraordinarily complex. Its officers were sophisticated international bankers whose apparent objective was to keep their affairs secret, to commit fraud on a massive scale, and to avoid detection."[7]

BCCI clients included the CIA and Afghanistan's heroin-smuggling mujahideen, Arab sheikhs, Iraq's Saddam Hussein,

$10,000 are made by multiple persons—nicknamed "smurfs"—or by one person on multiple days.

- *Offshore banking* involves deposits in countries that preserve client confidentiality with numbered accounts. Present-day centers of offshore banking include the Antilles, the Bahamas, Bahrain, the Cayman Islands, Hong Kong, Panama, and Singapore.
- *Underground banking* is popular in certain countries where alternative banking systems permit undocumented transactions. The best-known underground banks are found in Asia, including China's *fie chen* system and the *hawala* system widely used in India and Pakistan.

Panamanian dictator Manuel Noriega, leaders of Colombia's Medellín Cartel, and Israeli arms dealer Yair Klein, who sold the Medellín Cartel 500 machine guns in April 1989. One of those guns was used to murder Colombian presidential candidate Luis Galán Sarmiento four months later. Others were found after cartel kingpin Jose Rodriguez Gacha died in a shootout with Colombian federal agents.[8]

A U.S. Senate report published in 1992 called the BCCI's operations "the largest case of organized crime in history." In December 1991 bank officials pled guilty to various crimes, including seeking deposits of drug proceeds and laundering drug money, seeking deposits from U.S. tax evaders, using fronts to control American financial institutions, and creating false bank records to deceive regulators. Under terms of that plea agreement, all assets of the BCCI were subject to government seizure.[9]

Based on this case—and others, such as the scandals surrounding Rome's Vatican Bank and Castle Bank in the Bahamas—it seems clear that wealthy criminals labor around the clock to hide and launder their funds, ensuring that crime pays.

WHO LOSES?

While some observers regard drug offenses as victimless crimes, the same cannot be said of money laundering. Each year, criminals launder and hide an estimated $500 billion to $1 trillion dollars, belying claims that "crime does not pay."[10] That huge amount of cash—an underground economy, in fact—has major global impact in several spheres.

On a societal level, the obvious financial success of organized criminals encourages others to follow their example, dismissing lawful government as ineffective or corrupt. That influence extends from urban ghettos to corporate boardrooms, where fledgling felons claim that "everybody does it." When corruption is confirmed, by the dismissal or arrest of law enforcement officers caught taking bribes—or worse, in some cases—respect for law and order suffers major injury.

The economic effects of money laundering are likewise felt worldwide. Governments lose revenue when large amounts of untaxed cash are hidden and recycled. Banks that participate in money laundering, whether deliberately or otherwise, face a risk of collapse or seizure by police, jeopardizing the accounts of innocent depositors. Crises involving major banks tainted by crime threaten the survival of legitimate firms, and may topple state regimes. The owners and employees of companies used as money-laundering fronts may lose their livelihoods and homes.

Finally, laundered cash may threaten national or global security. Terrorists finance their activities with black-market cash, whether the campaign involves a drug cartel's attack on local authorities, or the globe-hopping raids of groups like Al-Qaeda. Aside from buying weapons and explosives, setting up guerrilla training camps, or shopping for nuclear warheads, criminals endanger a nation's security by corrupting law enforcement officers at every level. Bribed police are often negligent, and some have actively engaged in crimes of violence, such as contract murders.

FOLLOW THE MONEY

While money laundering per se is now illegal in the United States and 81 other countries, punishment requires legal evidence. Since money launderers operate worldwide, no single nation can defeat them. Global alliances created since the late 20th century include

- the *Financial Action Task Force on Money Laundering*, formed in 1989, including representatives of the United States and 31 other countries.[11]
- the *Caribbean Financial Action Task Force*, organized in a series of meetings between 1990 and 1992, with 30 member states.[12]
- the *Asian/Pacific Group on Money Laundering*, founded in 1997, presently including 40 member nations.[13]
- Europe's *Council of Europe Select Committee of Experts on the Evaluation of Anti-Money Laundering Measures*, established in 1997 with 28 permanent member nations.[14]
- the *Financial Action Task Force on Money Laundering in South America*, created in 2000 with 10 member nations.[15]
- the *Middle East and North Africa Financial Action Task Force*, founded in 2004 with 14 countries participating.[16]
- the *Eurasian Group on Combating Money Laundering and Financing of Terrorism*, established in 2004 with seven member nations and 16 more holding "observer" status.[17]

The DEA cooperates with all of these organizations and maintains 87 full-time foreign offices in 63 countries.[18] Its best-known victories over money launderers include the following:

- *José Franklin Jurado-Rodriguez,* a Harvard-educated economist from Colombia, used his skills to launder money for the Cali Cartel from 1984 to 1990. Living in Luxembourg, he transferred money through Panama and other nations. His downfall began when a neighbor complained of Jurado-Rodriguez using a noisy money-counter all night. Investigation led to Jurado-Rodriguez's 1992 arrest, with two accomplices. Aside from written records of his operation, officers seized $12 million in the United States, $16 million in Panama, and $30 million in Europe. Investigators traced Cali Cartel funds through 68 banks in nine countries, where Jurado-Rodriguez had more than 100 accounts. A Luxembourg court convicted Jurado-Rodriguez of money laundering in 1992, and he was later extradited to the United States, where he received an additional seven-year sentence.[19]

○ *Operation Dinero* (1992–1994) targeted Cali Cartel drug lords. Agents of the DEA's Atlanta, Georgia, office established a fake bank on the Caribbean island of Anguilla, inviting drug cartel leaders to launder their cash through a series of business "fronts." Cali mobsters used the DEA "bank" to sell three paintings by famed artists Pablo Picasso, Peter Rubens, and Joshua Reynolds, valued at more than $15 million. DEA and IRS agents seized the paintings in 1994, while making 116 arrests in four countries. Raiders also seized more than $90 million in cash and 9 tons of cocaine.[20]

○ *Operation Juno* (1995–1996) launched when 850 pounds of liquid cocaine was found in a shipment of frozen fish sent from Cartagena, Colombia, to Atlanta. Once again, DEA and IRS agents cooperated in a major "sting" operation, creating a false stockbroker's office in Atlanta to offer money-laundering services. Soon, investigators realized that they were dealing with members of the Cali Cartel and brokers for Colombia's Black Market Peso Exchange. Before the operation ended in September 1996, agents collected 59 cash shipments ranging from $100,000 to $500,000 each, and identified 59 accounts used for laundering money through 34 American banks. At the operation's climax, agents arrested 55 suspects and indicted five more residing in Colombia. They seized $36 million in cash, plus 7,922 pounds of cocaine.[21]

○ *Operation Double Trouble* (1999–2003), coordinated from Fort Lauderdale, Florida, spanned five U.S. states and two continents as the investigation progressed. The initial target was Ivan Henao, a Colombian drug trafficker and money launderer whose syndicate was one of 53 criminal organizations listed as Consolidated Priority Organization Targets. DEA and IRS agents determined that 18 drug distribution networks used Henao's money-laundering service to launder at least $30 million between June 1999 and August 2003, when authorities dismantled the syndicate. On August 29, 2003, DEA headquarters announced 55 arrests and the seizure of 36 accounts in 11 Colombian banks. Raiders also confiscated

$12.8 million in cash, 777 pounds of cocaine, and 46 pounds of heroin.[22]

- *Gilberto and Miguel Rodriguez-Orjuela,* Cali Cartel leaders, were indicted on money-laundering charges in March 2004. Based on DEA investigations, the brothers were charged with conspiring to hide more than $1 billion in drug money from authorities in the United States and Colombia. Both were already in custody—Miguel arrested in 1995, Gilberto captured in March 2003—but extradition still took time. Colombia extradited Gilberto in December 2004, and Miguel followed in March 2005. Both finally pled guilty on multiple felony charges, receiving 30-year prison terms in September 2006.[23]

- *Operation Money Clip* (2003–2004) began with a routine traffic stop in Texas. Police found a large amount of cash in the reckless driver's car and reported their discovery to DEA agents as suspected drug money. Before the operation ended in October 2004, the DEA's Special Operations Division had completed 43 separate investigations spanning the United States. At its conclusion, the campaign produced 83 arrests and seized $4.4 million in cash, 39,265 pounds of marijuana, 5,557 pounds of cocaine, 74 pounds of crystallized methamphetamine, 2 pounds of heroin, 45 vehicles, and five homes. DEA spokesmen told reporters:

  > Operation Money Clip clearly illustrates how money fuels the drug trade, and attacking these illicit profits is the key to dismantling drug organizations. . . . This operation ensures that these drug traffickers will never do business on American streets again and proves that, in order to defeat these large criminal organizations, law enforcement must be coordinated and united.[24]

- *Operation Choque* (2004) targeted Mexican money broker and narcotics trafficker Saul "The Engineer" Saucedo-Chaidez. His syndicate imported 1,320 pounds of cocaine per week from Mexico and laundered $43 million per year. The final DEA crackdown produced 60 arrests, plus seizure of $10.4 million in cash, 5,100 pounds of cocaine, and 521 pounds of marijuana.[25]

- The *Money Trail Initiative* was announced by DEA headquarters in July 2005. At that press conference, Administrator Karen Tandy told the media, "While money is the main motivation for drug traffickers, it is also their number one vulnerability. In this initiative, we followed the money trail from several cash seizures in the U.S. around the Western Hemisphere." By the time the new campaign was publicized, it had already logged 230 arrests, with seizures including $28 million in cash, 37,055 pounds of marijuana, and 3,478 pounds of cocaine.[26]

- *Operation Long Wine* (2005) targeted a Mexican drug cartel involved in smuggling cocaine and methamphetamine, as well as large-scale money laundering. Its culmination produced indictments of 33 suspects, 28 of whom were captured in October 2005. DEA raiders also seized $8 million in cash, 1,302 pounds of cocaine, and 40 pounds of crystallized methamphetamine.[27]

- In January 2006 *Martin Tremblay,* a Canadian who served as president and managing director of Dominion Investments, was arrested in the Bahamas. Between 1998 and 2005, Tremblay laundered at least $1 billion for various criminal clients, collecting large fees in the process. Dominion's Web site advertised the company as a "leader in the offshore financial services" market, offering its clients "the knowledge and expertise they need to effectively use international tax planning, asset protection, and other wealth preservation techniques." According to the indictment, Dominion's accounts contained $50 million earned from tax evasion and wire fraud, $3 million from the sale of illegal GHB kits (powdered chemicals mixed with tap water to produce the "date-rape drug" gamma-hydroxybutyrate), plus millions more derived from stock fraud and drug trafficking. Tremblay pled guilty on one count of money laundering in February 2007 and received a four-year sentence.[28]

- *Operation Watusi* (2006) was a joint DEA-FBI-Customs campaign targeting a drug network based in Medellín, Colombia, led by fugitive felon Luis Peña-Peña. Multiple indictments charged Peña-Peña with smuggling cocaine from Colombia to Puerto Rico, laundering the proceeds, and kidnapping a U.S. Customs agent for $2 million ransom in December 2005. Operation Watusi produced 56 arrests, plus seizure of various bank accounts containing a total of $3.1 million, 4,180 pounds of cocaine, and six boats used to ferry drugs around the Caribbean.[29]

○ DEA Administrator Tandy announced the world-record seizure of $207 million in drug money in March 2007. Tandy told reporters that the cash was seized from chemical brokers who supplied Mexican drug cartels with material required to manufacture methamphetamine, earmarked for sale in the United States. According to Tandy, the Mexican cartels produce 80 percent of all illegal methamphetamine sold and consumed in America.[30]

○ The February 2007 arrest of *Naresh Kumar Patel*, an international money launderer based in Dubai, United Arab Emirates (UAE), was a significant law enforcement achievement. A joint investigation conducted by the DEA and foreign authorities revealed that Patel laundered millions of dollars in drug money through 16 identified bank accounts. Following his arrest, with 39 accomplices, Patel admitted his guilt and acknowledged that most of the money he "washed" was derived from drug trafficking.[31]

○ In February 2008 a joint force of DEA and IRS agents arrested Diamond Golf Company (DGC) chief executive officer *Peter Carlo Mertens* and his wife, along with two employees, on charges of running a checks-for-cash scheme to launder revenue earned from marijuana trafficking. According to the indictment, the defendants laundered at least $500,000 for pot grower Ian Mahon, paying Mahon as an "independent contractor" although he never worked for DGC. Mahon pled guilty to drug trafficking and money laundering in 2005, after DEA agents raided several of his California marijuana "grow houses."[32]

○ In March 2009 indictments of six Colombian nationals who ran the *DMG Group*—a money-laundering network that took its name from the initials of ringleader David Murcia Guzmán—were issued. The DMG Group was created in 2003, "as a vehicle . . . through which customers could purchase pre-paid debit cards to purchase electronics and other items at retail stores operated by DMG." The purchases were made with drug money collected from 400,000 customers as of 2008. DMG laundered that money through

David Murcia Guzmán, money launderer and former head of the DMG Group, is escorted by Colombian police officers at the military airport in Bogotá, Colombia. *(John Viscaino/Reuters/Corbis)*

Colombia's Black Market Peso Exchange and bought American real estate through the Merrill Lynch investment firm using an account registered to "Blackstone International Development."[33]

PERSISTENT THREATS

Despite such victories, money laundering continues, supporting all forms of organized crime. The black-market cash equips criminal syndicates with weapons, corrupts public officials, and finances acts of terrorism worldwide. In January 2006 the DEA's Public Affairs Division released the federal government's first interagency Money Laundering Threat Assessment. The document emerged from a cooperative effort by the Departments of Justice, Treasury, and Homeland Security; the U.S. Postal Service; and the Federal Reserve System's board of directors.

OPERATION MALLORCA

While some criminals launder cash through licensed banks and legitimate companies, others prefer secret networks such as Colombia's Black Market Peso Exchange (BMPE), which was created in the 1980s for the benefit of drug cartels. Smugglers are paid for their drugs in the currency of nations where they sell them—dollars, francs, euros, and so on—but cartel leaders can only spend pesos in Colombia. Peso brokers purchase foreign money at a discount, which becomes their profit, while drug traffickers are free to spend their "clean" money at home.

In June 2005 DEA Administrator Karen Tandy announced the successful conclusion of "Operation Mallorca," a 27-month investigation of money laundering by BMPE brokers. The campaign produced 36 arrests in the United States and Colombia. Raiders also seized $7.2 million in cash, plus 21,650 pounds of marijuana, 2,083 pounds of cocaine, and 15 pounds of heroin.[34]

As Tandy described the operation to reporters:

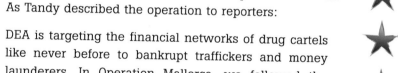

> DEA is targeting the financial networks of drug cartels like never before to bankrupt traffickers and money launderers. In Operation Mallorca, we followed the money around the globe and into the hands of major Colombian drug traffickers. We've shown the Black Market Peso Exchange for what it is—the largest known drug money laundering mechanism in the Western Hemisphere. DEA showed today that traffickers can move their money around the world, but we will track it down.[35]

Tandy noted that DEA raids had stripped drug traffickers of $500 million in profits during 2004 alone, but much remained to be done. "We know," she said, "that major drug traffickers have insulated themselves from their drug distribution networks, but remain closely linked to the proceeds of their trade. Operation Mallorca is a testament to our focus on the financial side of the drug business."[36]

(continues)

(continued)

Evidence gathered during Operation Mallorca documented 68 separate transfers of cash exceeding $12 million, conducted in 16 U.S. cities and 13 foreign countries. The transactions included 300 wire transfers to 200 bank accounts with 170 separate owners. In addition to tracing drug money, Operation Mallorca identified 13 different trafficking groups in Colombia, formed since the breakdown of major cartels in the 1990s.[37]

Despite those arrests and the adverse exposure, the Black Market Peso Exchange remained active in 2009, still serving its criminal clients worldwide.[38] As long as felons reap huge profits from illegal enterprises, they will find accountants, bankers, and investors to assist them.

Donald Semesky Jr., the DEA's chief of financial operations, told reporters:

From Hawalas to the Black Market Peso Exchange to the bulk smuggling of cash across our nation's borders, DEA is targeting drug traffickers' tainted profits like never before. Last year, DEA seized a record $1.9 billion from the pockets of greed-driven drug traffickers worldwide. The money trail that leads to drug traffickers' wallets is the same trail that will lead to their ultimate demise.[39]

Chris Swecker, assistant director of the FBI's Criminal Investigation Division, added, "One of our critical missions is to protect the integrity of our financial system. This comprehensive assessment is a significant step towards stemming the flow of illicit proceeds into the United States and insuring that our financial institutions are not utilized to facilitate terrorism or criminal activities."[40]

Fallen
Soldiers

Post, Texas

Spencer Stafford joined the U.S. Treasury Department's Bureau of Narcotics after graduating from pharmacy school in New York. Rather than filling prescriptions in a local drugstore, he preferred to battle crime by pursuing drug traffickers. He served at bureau offices in New York, Georgia, and Florida before he was assigned to Fort Worth, Texas, in 1931.

Then, as today, the states bordering Mexico were prime territory for smugglers bringing illegal drugs into the United States. In 1934 Inspector Stafford learned that one such operation was based in Post, Texas, where it enjoyed protection from corrupt police.

The town of Post was founded in 1907 by cereal magnate Charles Post, whose famous brands today include Grape-Nuts, Pebbles, Post Alpha-Bits and many others. Post conceived the town that bears his name as a utopian community devoid of crime, but Prohibition doomed that dream. Sheriff W. F. Cato and his deputy, Tom Morgan, went beyond the era's norm of accepting bribes to ignore liquor smuggling. Rather than simply turning a blind eye to "victimless" crime, they collaborated with narcotics smugglers and dealers.

Two of Post's drug traffickers were physician V.A. Hartman and veterinarian L. W. Kitchen. Inspector Stafford discovered that both doctors used their medical licenses and connections to purchase and transfer drugs on behalf of criminal dealers. He visited Dr. Kitchen's veterinary clinic on February 7, 1935, and emerged to find Sheriff Cato waiting outside, with

THE DEA MUSEUM

The DEA's Wall of Honor is located at the agency's museum and visitors center, created in 1976 as part of the federal government's bicentennial celebration, "to educate the American public on the history of drugs, drug addiction and drug law enforcement in the United States through engaging and state-of-the-art exhibits, displays, interactive stations and educational outreach programs."[1] It is operated by the DEA Educational Foundation and offers various exhibits detailing both the agency's history and the impact of drugs on American society.

As this book went to press, the museum's exhibits included "Illegal Drugs in America: A Modern History," "Target America: Opening Eyes to the Damage Drugs Cause," and "Good Medicine, Bad Behavior: Drug Diversion in America." The DEA's artifact collection includes more than 2000 objects ranging from old patent medicine bottles to more modern drug smuggling containers, and some 5,000 photographs taken since the 19th century. "Virtual exhibits" are also accessible online at the DEA's Web site.[2]

The DEA Museum & Visitors Center is located in Arlington, Virginia, across the street from the Pentagon City Mall. It

Deputy Morgan. Before Stafford could draw his weapon, Sheriff Cato opened fire on him with a submachine gun, killing Stafford instantly.

While similar crimes had gone unpunished in the past, a new law passed by Congress in May 1934 made it a federal crime to kill U.S. government agents in the course of their official duties. Agents soon arrested Cato and Morgan, winning convictions in federal court on the first application of the new law. Doctors Hartman and Kitchen were also prosecuted and imprisoned, for violation of federal narcotics laws.[3]

PERILOUS DUTY

The Wall of Honor at the DEA's museum lists 59 persons who have lost their lives since the agency was formed in July 1973, including 36 field

charges no admission fee and is open to the public four days per week, Tuesday through Friday, from 10:00 A.M. to 4:00 P.M. Advance reservations are required for parties of 15 persons or more.

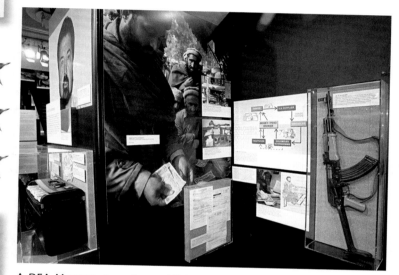

A DEA Museum traveling exhibit entitled "Target America: Traffickers, Terrorists and You" is displayed in Times Square in New York City. *(Katy Winn/Corbis)*

investigators, 12 members of other law enforcement agencies who died while working with the DEA, and 11 civilian employees.[4] Another 19 deaths named belong to individuals slain while employed by the DEA's predecessor organizations.

EARLY MARTYRS

The DEA did not exist until July 1973, but its museum honors federal drug-enforcement agents killed in the line of duty over five preceding decades. They include the following individuals:

- *Stafford Beckett* and *Charles Wood*, agents with the Bureau of Internal Revenue's Border Department, were killed by whiskey smugglers during a raid at a ranch near El Paso, Texas, on March 22, 1921. During the two preceding weeks, bootleggers had engaged in seven shootouts with federal officers. Agent Beckett himself had killed a suspected smuggler the day before he was murdered.[5]

o *Joseph Floyd,* a Prohibition agent, was slain during a raid in Houston, Texas, on May 17, 1922. Floyd was shot from ambush before he could draw his weapon or remove the search warrant from his pocket.[6]

o *James Williams,* also a Prohibition agent, was killed while grappling with a Chicago bootlegger on October 16, 1924. Narcotics Agent George Howard joined in the arrest, which soon became a brawl, and accidentally fired his pistol during the struggle, striking Williams in the head.[7]

o *James Brown* was shot three times and killed instantly by a suspected opium trafficker near Isleton, California, on June 7, 1928.[8]

o *James Kerrigan* was badly injured when he fell during a raid on a Newark, New Jersey, opium den on September 28, 1928. Kerrigan returned to work after that accident, but internal injuries required surgery three months later. He died from complications of that operation on December 27, 1928.[9]

o *Anker Bangs,* an FBN agent in St. Paul, Minnesota, was killed by a drug addict during an undercover investigation of a local opium den on September 24, 1950.[10]

o *Wilson Shee,* an FBN agent in San Francisco, was slain by a deranged, drug-addicted confidential informant on December 12, 1957.[11]

o *Mansel Burrell,* an undercover FBN agent, was killed by heroin smugglers in Gary, Indiana, on December 19, 1967.[12]

o *Gene Clifton,* a local police officer in Palo Alto, California, was shot while engaged in a joint raid with Bureau of Narcotics and Dangerous Drugs (BNDD) agents on October 1, 1971. Clifton died from his wounds on November 19.[13]

o *Frank Tummillo,* an undercover BNDD agent, was shot and killed on October 12, 1972, while negotiating purchase of a cocaine shipment from two suspects in New York City. BNDD Agent *Thomas*

Devine was wounded in the same incident; he was left paralyzed and died of complications from his wounds in 1982.[14]

- *Richard Heath Jr.* was the first U.S. narcotics agent killed outside the country. Heath was shot during an undercover operation at Aruba, in the Netherlands Antilles, on February 22, 1973. Physicians in Aruba mistook him for one of the drug traffickers and denied him proper treatment. Heath died on April 1, after his transfer to a hospital in Quito, Ecuador.[15]

DANGEROUS SKIES

No single DEA division has claimed more lives than the agency's aviation program, which today consists of nearly 100 aircraft and 125 agent-pilots.[16] Aside from transporting DEA officials and equipment, agency pilots also play a critical role in many surveillance and drug-interdiction campaigns. Those who have died while flying in the DEA's service include the following:

- *Agents Ralph Shaw* and *James Lunn* were killed when their plane crashed north of Guadalajara, Mexico, on May 14, 1976. At the time, the agents were engaged in surveillance supporting a Mexican campaign to eradicate opium poppies. The crash occurred after they flew into a box canyon at low altitude.[17]

- *Agent Larry Carwell* was killed on January 9, 1984, when his helicopter crashed at sea, off the Bahamas, during a search for cocaine smugglers. Nine months later, Agent Carwell was awarded the International Narcotic Enforcement Officers Association's Medal of Valor "for having performed his duty at a personal risk of life."[18]

- *Agent Rickie Finley* was killed when his plane crashed into a mountain near Tingo Maria, Peru, on May 20, 1989. Finley was on his second tour of duty in "Operation Snowcap," targeting Peruvian cocaine growers. Today, the DEA's field office in Detroit bears his name.[19]

- *Agent Alan Winn* was killed on August 13, 1991, when his helicopter crashed during a marijuana-spotting mission in Hawaii. The crash was caused by an engine malfunction.[20]

- *Agents Frank Hernandez Jr., Jay Seale, Meredith Thompson, Juan Vars*, and *Frank Wallace Jr.* lost their lives when their plane crashed near Santa Lucia, Peru, on August 27, 1994. Their flight, like the one that killed Agent Finley five years earlier, was part of "Operation Snowcap."[21]
- *Pilot instructor Larry Steilen,* a civilian employee of the DEA who had flown support missions for Operation Snowcap in Peru, was killed when his helicopter crashed during a training exercise at Fort Worth, Texas, on September 25, 1998.[22]
- *Agent Terry Loftus* died while en route from Chicago to St. Louis on May 28, 2004. Soon after takeoff, Loftus reported engine failure in his Cessna aircraft. He crashed while trying to land in a field near Homer Glen, Illinois.[23]

DARKEST HOURS

The Peruvian airplane crash that killed five DEA agents in 1994 was not the agency's worst moment. That occurred 20 years earlier, on August 5, 1974, when the DEA's field office in Miami, Florida, collapsed without warning, killing seven persons and trapping several others in the wreckage. Witnesses initially suspected an explosion or an earthquake, but subsequent investigation blamed old and faulty construction materials. The building had been erected in 1925, and underwent a full engineering inspection in 1968, but experts determined that salt and sand mixed with resurfacing materials had eroded the six-inch concrete floor or the structure's rooftop parking facility.[24]

Those killed in the building's collapse included secretary Mary Keehan, Agents Nickolas Fragos and Charles Mann, fiscal assistant Anna Pope, secretary Anna Mounger, supervisory clerk-typist Martha Skeels, and clerk-typist Mary Sullivan. All are memorialized on the DEA's Wall of Honor.[25]

Another disaster rocked the DEA on April 19, 1995, when a terrorist's truck bomb exploded outside the Alfred P. Murrah Federal Building in Oklahoma City. The blast killed at least 168 persons—a severed leg remains unidentified—including five employed by the DEA. They included Agent Kenneth McCullough, office assistant Carrol Fields, and three persons working under temporary contracts with the DEA:

Rona Chafey, a dispatcher for the Cleveland County Sheriff's Office, assigned to a DEA multiagency task force; and two DynCorp legal technicians, Shelly Bland and Carrie Lenz.[26]

The Oklahoma City bomb was built by two right-wing extremists, Timothy McVeigh and Terry Nichols. McVeigh was convicted on 11 counts of murder in June 1997 and sentenced to die. He was executed by lethal injection on June 11, 2001. Nichols was convicted on 161 murder counts in May 2004 and received 161 consecutive life sentences. Michael Fortier, a friend of the bombers who had advance knowledge of their plans and failed to warn authorities, received a 12-year sentence in May 1998. He was paroled in January 2006 and entered the federal witness protection program.

CASUALTIES OF WAR

The best-known DEA casualties are agents killed by felons in the line of duty. While the DEA mourns all its losses equally, these are the cases that make headlines and sometimes inspire films or novels. Frontline victims of the DEA's drug war include the following individuals:

- *Agent Emir Benitez* was shot while working undercover on a Florida cocaine investigation, on August 9, 1973. Benitez is the DEA's first martyr, killed one month after the agency's creation.[27]
- *Agent Larry Wallace* was shot during an undercover heroin investigation on the island of Guam, on December 19, 1975. Wallace and another DEA agent were transporting a handcuffed prisoner when the prisoner drew a hidden gun and shot both agents, killing Wallace.[28]
- *Agent Octavio Gonzalez* was the DEA's top-ranking officer in Bogotá, Colombia, in 1976. On December 13 of that year, Gonzales was shot and killed in his office by an informant-turned-hitman. The gunman later committed suicide in custody.[29]
- *Agent Enrique Camarena Salazar* was kidnapped and tortured to death by Mexican drug traffickers in February 1985.
- *Agent William Ramos* was shot while trying to arrest marijuana dealer Felipe Molina-Uribe during an undercover operation in Las

Milpas, Texas, on December 31, 1986. Molina-Uribe suffered a leg wound in that incident, and later received a life sentence.[30]

- *Agent Raymond Stastny* was shot in Buckhead, Georgia, less than three weeks after Agent Ramos died in Texas. Stastny was involved in an undercover operation when a suspect shot him on January 20, 1987. Other officers killed the gunman. Stastny survived until January 26.[31]

- *Agents George Montoya* and *Paul Seema* were shot in Los Angeles on February 5, 1988, during an undercover operation. The agents

OPERATION LEYENDA

Enrique Camarena Salazar—"Kiki" to his friends—was born on July 26, 1947, in Mexicali, Mexico. In 1956 his family moved across the border to Calexico, California, where Camarena attended high school and became a naturalized U.S. citizen. He served two years in the Marine Corps (1972–1974), and then worked as a firefighter and police officer before joining the DEA. In 1981 Camarena was assigned to the DEA's office in Guadalajara, where he investigated Mexican drug cartels.

On February 7, 1985, Camarena left work to meet his wife for lunch but never kept their date. Outside the DEA's office, four men grabbed Camarena and forced him into a car. Hours later, gunmen also kidnapped Alfredo Zavala Avelar, a pilot employed with Mexico's Agriculture Department, who worked on antidrug campaigns. A widespread manhunt began after Camarena's wife reported him missing. One of those questioned was Rafael Caro Quintero, a founder and leader of the Guadalajara Cartel. Caro fled to Costa Rica on February 9, after questioning by Mexican federal officers.

On March 5 police found the bodies of Camarena and Zavala near Michoacan, Mexico. Both had been tortured, then bludgeoned, buried, and later exhumed to be dumped outside Michoacan. The investigation—dubbed "Operation Leyenda"—shifted to a search for the killers.

were negotiating purchase of a heroin shipment from Taiwanese smugglers when the traffickers drew guns and tried to rob them of $80,000. Agent Montoya was killed instantly, but Agent Seema survived until February 6. DEA agents and local police killed two of the gunmen and wounded a third after a high-speed chase. The wounded killer, William Wang, later received a sentence of life imprisonment without parole. Accomplice Michael Chia, though not present at the shooting, was convicted of murder in 1988. A federal court overturned that verdict in February 2002,

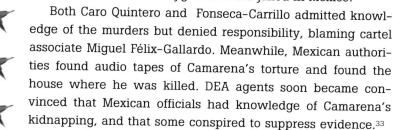

On March 14 Mexican *federales* arrested five Jalisco State Police officers. One died under interrogation, while the other four confessed to participating in the slayings and named other suspects, including Rafael Caro Quintero and longtime partner Ernesto Fonseca-Carrillo. Eleven more suspects were jailed on March 17. Caro Quintero was captured with seven associates by DEA agents and Costa Rican police on April 4. Costa Rica deported the suspects to Mexico on April 5. Two days later, Fonseca and several bodyguards were jailed in Mexico.[32]

Both Caro Quintero and Fonseca-Carrillo admitted knowledge of the murders but denied responsibility, blaming cartel associate Miguel Félix-Gallardo. Meanwhile, Mexican authorities found audio tapes of Camarena's torture and found the house where he was killed. DEA agents soon became convinced that Mexican officials had knowledge of Camarena's kidnapping, and that some conspired to suppress evidence.[33]

Operation Leyenda ultimately produced more than two dozen arrests on various charges related to the Camarena-Zavala murders. A dozen defendants were convicted in Mexico, including Caro Quintero and Fonseca-Carrillo, who received 40-year sentences. Several others faced trial in the United States. One of those, Dr. Humberto Álvarez-Macháin, was kidnapped from Mexico by bounty hunters for trial on charges that he kept Camarena alive with drugs during torture. Jurors acquitted him, but his lawsuit against the U.S. government was dismissed.[34]

DEA Agent Enrique Camarena Salazar was tortured and murdered by Mexican police officers and agents of the Guadalajara Cartel in Mexico in February 1985. The search for his killers, dubbed "Operation Leyenda," led to the arrest of more than two dozen people on various charges in connection with the murder. *(AP Photo)*

but he was once again convicted at a second trial, in September 2005.[35]

- *Agent Everett Hatcher* was shot by Mafia-affiliated drug dealer Costabile Farace during an undercover cocaine buy on Staten Island, New York, on February 28, 1989. Authorities found Farace dead in Brooklyn on November 18, 1989, apparently executed by members of his own crime family.[36]

- *Agent Richard Fass* was shot on June 30, 1994, during an undercover methamphetamine investigation in Glendale, Arizona. The killers escaped into Mexico, but their leader, Agustín Vasquez Mendoza, was extradited for trial in January 2005. In November 2006 he received a 71-year sentence for murder, kidnapping, aggravated assault, attempted armed robbery, and conspiracy. The actual killers were also apprehended. Two received life sentences and a third cooperated with authorities in exchange for leniency.[37]

Chronology

1927	**April**: Bureau of Prohibition created
1930	**June**: Federal Bureau of Narcotics (FBN) created
1966	**February**: Bureau of Drug Abuse Control (BDAC) replaces the FBN
1968	**August**: Bureau of Narcotics and Dangerous Drugs (BNDD) replaces BDAC
1972	**January**: Office of Drug Abuse Law Enforcement (ODALE) created
1973	**July**: DEA created, merging the BNDD and ODALE
	October: Unified Intelligence Division organized
	November: First DEA Special Agent Basic Training Class completed
1974	**August**: Seven die in collapse of the DEA Miami office building
	November: First DEA Intelligence Analyst Training School convened
1975	**April**: First DEA Central Tactical Unit created
1976	**October**: DEA Office of Compliance and Regulatory Affairs established
1978	**April**: First DEA Clandestine Methamphetamine Laboratory School established
1979	**July**: First major cocaine shootout on U.S. soil, in Miami
1982	**January**: Vice President's Task Force on South Florida organized
	March: Pablo Escobar elected to Colombian Congress; DEA initiates high school drug-education programs nationwide

	October: Comprehensive Crime Control Act passed by Congress
1985	**January**: First extradition of Colombian traffickers to the United States
	February: DEA Agent Enrique Camarena Salazar murdered in Mexico
	November: Cartel-allied guerrillas storm Colombia's Palace of Justice
1986	**February**: DEA informant Barry Seal assassinated in Louisiana
	March: Controlled Substance Analogue Enforcement Act bans "designer" drugs
	October: President Reagan signs the Anti-Drug Abuse Act
	November: Medellín Cartel leaders indicted in the United States
1987	**February**: Carlos Lehder captured and extradited
	March: 25 Mafia members convicted in "Pizza Connection" heroin trial
	June: Colombia annuls U.S. extradition treaty
1988	**February**: Manuel Noriega indicted in the United States
	November: Office of National Drug Control Policy created
	August: Medellín Cartel declares war on Colombia's government
	September: Sylmar, California, cocaine seizure (21.5 tons)
1990	**January**: Manuel Noriega surrenders in Panama
	June: New Colombian constitution bans extradition
	November: Mexican soldiers massacre federal drug agents
	August: DEA Intelligence Division created
1993	**December:** Pablo Escobar killed in Colombia
1994	**August**: Five DEA agents die in Peruvian airplane crash
1995	**February**: Drug Trafficking Act of 1994 comes into force
	April: Five DEA agents die in bombing of Oklahoma City's federal building
2006	**January**: Smugglers' tunnel from Tijuana to California discovered

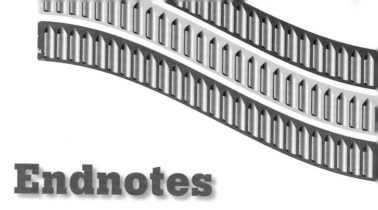

Endnotes

Introduction

1. NPR, "Timeline: America's War on Drugs," http://www.npr.org/templates/story/story.php?storyId=9252490 (Accessed August 22, 2009).
2. Gary Fields, "White House czar calls for end to 'War on Drugs,'" *Wall Street Journal,* May 14, 2009.
3. Pew Research Center for the People and the Press, February 14–19, 2001, http://www.pollingreport.com/drugs.htm (Accessed August 22, 2009).
4. Office of National Drug Control Policy, http://www.whitehouse-drugpolicy.gov/ publications/drugfact/american_users_spend/section1.html (Accessed August 22, 2009).
5. Ibid.
6. Bureau of Justice Statistics, http://bjs.ojp.usdoj.gov/content/glance/drug.cfm (Accessed August 25, 2010).
7. Ibid.
8. Ibid.
9. Office of Applied Studies, "National Survey on Drug Use & Health," http://www.oas.samhsa.gov/nhsda.htm (Accessed August 22, 2009).
10. Drug War Clock, http://www.drugsense.org/wodclock.htm (Accessed August 22, 2009).
11. DrugWarFacts.org, "Drug Interdiction," http://www.drugwarfacts.org/cms/?q=node/50 (Accessed August 22, 2009).
12. Bureau of Justice Statistics, http://bjs.ojp.usdoj.gov/index.cfm?ty=kfa (Accessed August 25, 2010).

Chapter 1

1. DEA, "Hundreds of Alleged Sinaloa Cartel Members and Associates Arrested in Nationwide Takedown of Mexican Drug Traffickers," http://www.justice.gov/dea/pubs/states/newsrel/2009/la022509.html (Accessed August 22, 2009).
2. Ibid.
3. "Mexico drug lord on Forbes rich list with $1 billion," Reuters, March 11, 2009, http://www.reuters.com/article/lifestyleMolt/idUSTRE52A7QM20090311 (Accessed August 22, 2009).
4. "Drug-related killings in Mexico on course to top last year's numbers," CNN, July 9, 2009, http://www.cnn.com/2009/WORLD/americas/07/09/mexico.drug.violence/ index.html (Accessed August 22, 2009).
5. DEA, "Hundreds of Alleged Sinaloa Cartel Members and Associates Arrested in Nationwide Takedown of Mexican Drug Traf-

fickers," http://www.justice.gov/dea/pubs/states/newsrel/2009/la022509.html (Accessed August 22, 2009).

6. DEA, "Wall of Honor," http://www.justice.gov/dea/agency/10_list.htm (Accessed August 22, 2009).

7. Officer Down Memorial Page, http://www.odmp.org/agency/1050-united-states-department-of-justice---drug-enforcement-administration-u.s.-government (Accessed August 22, 2009).

8. DEA, "DEA Demand Reduction Program," http://www.justice.gov/dea/programs/demand.htm (Accessed August 22, 2009).

9. DEA, "Drug Enforcement Administration," http://www.justice.gov/dea/pubs/history/1970-1975.pdf (Accessed August 22, 2009).

10. Officer Down Memorial Page.

11. DEA, "Speaking Out Against Drug Legalization," http://www.justice.gov/dea/demand/speakout/index.html (Accessed August 22, 2009).

12. DEA, "Drug Enforcement Administration," http://www.justice.gov/dea/pubs/history/1970-1975.pdf (Accessed August 22, 2009).

13. DEA, "DEA Mission Statement," http://www.justice.gov/dea/agency/mission.htm (Accessed August 22, 2009).

14. DEA, "Stats and Facts," http://www.justice.gov/dea/statistics.html (Accessed August 22, 2009).

15. Criminal Justice Policy Foundation, http://cjpf.org/comments PEWdrugpoll03-21-01.html (Accessed August 22, 2009).

16. Officer Down Memorial Page.

17. Constitution of the United States, Article I, Section 9.

18. General Accounting Office press release (January 4, 2005), http://proxychi.baremetal.com/csdp.org/research/303495.pdf (Accessed August 22, 2009).

19. Office of National Drug Control Policy, "Policy," http://www.whitehousedrugpolicy.gov/policy/index.html (Accessed August 22, 2009).

20. General Accounting Office press release (January 4, 2005).

21. DEA, "DEA Mission Statement," http://www.justice.gov/dea/agency/mission.htm (Accessed August 22, 2009).

22. DEA, "Drug Questionnaire," http://www.justice.gov/dea/job/agent/bef_drugQuest.html (Accessed August 22, 2009).

23. "FBI may relax drug use hiring policy," Associated Press, October 10, 2005, http://www.highbeam.com/doc/1P1-113971551.html (Accessed August 22, 2009).

24. DEA, "Programs and Operations," http://www.justice.gov/dea/programs/progs.htm (Accessed August 22, 2009).

25. Ibid.

26. Officer Down Memorial Page.

27. DEA, "Programs and Operations," http://www.justice.gov/dea/programs/progs.htm (Accessed August 22, 2009).

28. Office of National Drug Control Policy, "High Intensity Drug Trafficking Areas," http://www.whitehousedrugpolicy.gov/hidta/index.html (Accessed August 22, 2009).

29. Ibid.

30. Ibid.

31. Ibid.

Chapter 2

1. Drug Enforcement Administration, "Operation Green Air," http://www.justice.gov/dea/major/greenair.htm (Accessed August 23, 2009).

2. Tim Steller, "Mexican drug runners may have used C-130 from Arizona," *Arizona Daily Star*, April 15, 1998.

3. DEA, "Operation Green Air," http://www.justice.gov/dea/major/greenair.htm (Accessed August 23, 2009).

4. DEA, "Over 100 Arrested in Multi-Million Dollar Marijuana Smuggling Operation," http://www.justice.gov/dea/pubs/pressrel/pr041300.htm (Accessed August 23, 2009).

5. Cannabis.net, "Cannabis Chronology," http://www.cannabis.net/marijuana-timeline.html (Accessed August 23, 2009).

6. Ibid.; Library of Congress, *The Writings of George Washington*, Volume 33, page 270.

7. "Cannabis Chronology."

8. Ibid.

9. Charles Whitebread, "The history of the non-medical use of drugs in the United States," Drug Library, http://druglibrary.org/schaffer/HISTORY/whiteb1.htm (Accessed August 23, 2009).

10. "Cannabis in Africa," UKCIA.org, http://www.ukcia.org/research/Geopolitics/CannabisInAfrica.html (Accessed August 23, 2009); Karen Lotter, "Cannabis Tourism in South Africa," (September 22, 2007), http://south-africa-travel.suite101.com/article.cfm/cannabis_tourism_to_south_africa (Accessed August 23, 2009).

11. "Cannabis in Africa."

12. "Cannabis in Africa."

13. Morocco: Illegal Drugs, http://www.magharebia.com/cocoon/awi/xhtml1/en_GB/keyword/issue/illegaldrugs (Accessed August 23, 2009).

14. Alabi Uwiagbo, "NDLEA: A Decade of Drug Law Enforcement in Nigeria," http://againstbabangida.

com/docs/gloriaokon.pdf (Accessed August 23, 2009); "Nigeria marijuana seeds," Mary Jane's Garden, http://www.maryjanesgarden.com/nigeria.php (Accessed August 23, 2009); "Nigerian Marijuana," Marijuana Strains, www.marijuanastrains.com/nigeriastrains.html (Accessed August 23, 2009).

15. CIA World Factbook, https://www.cia.gov/library/publications/the-world-factbook/geos/cg.html (Accessed August 23, 2009).

16. "UNODC in Eastern Africa," United Nations Office on Drugs and Crime, http://www.unodc.org/easternafrica (Accessed August 23, 2009).

17. DEA, "Foreign Field Divisions," http://www.justice.gov/dea/pubs/international/foreign.html (Accessed August 23, 2009).

18. Harry Anslinger and Courtney Ryley Cooper, "Marijuana, Assassin of Youth," *American Magazine* (July 1937), http://www.redhousebooks.com/galleries/assassin.htm (Accessed August 23, 2009).

19. "Cannabis Chronology."

20. Ibid.

21. "13 Legal Marijuana States," ProCon.org, http://medicalmarijuana.procon.org/viewresource.asp?resourceID=000881 (Accessed August 23, 2009); "DEA raids 10 Los Angeles medical marijuana clinics," Fox News, July 26, 2007, http://www.foxnews.com/story/0,2933,290852,00.html (Accessed August 23, 2009).

22. DEA, "Stats & Facts," http://www.justice.gov/dea/statistics.html#seizures (Accessed August 23, 2009).

23. "Top 10 Pros and Cons: Should marijuana be a medical option?" ProCon.org, http://medicalmarijuana.procon.org/viewresource.

asp?resourceID=000141 (Accessed August 23, 2009).

24. Ibid.

25. Ibid.

26. Alex Johnson, "DEA to halt medical marijuana raids," MSNBC, http://www.msnbc.msn.com/id/29433.

27. DrugWarFacts.Org, "Marijuana Facts," http://drugwarfacts.org/cms/?q=node/53 (Accessed August 23, 2009).

28. "Cannabis Chronology."

29. United Nations Office on Drugs and Crime, *World Drug Report 2006*, Vol. 1 (Vienna, Austria: United Nations, 2006), 23.

30. Lloyd Johnson, Patrick O'Malley, Jerald Bachman, and John Schulenberg, *Monitoring the Future National Survey Results on Drug Use, 1975–2005: Volume I, Secondary School Students* (Bethesda, Md.: National Institute on Drug Abuse, 2006), 401.708 (Accessed August 23, 2009).

Chapter 3

1. Mark Stevenson, "Top Mexico cops charged with favoring drug cartel," ABC News, January 24, 2009, http://www.thefreelibrary.com/Top+Mexico+cops+charged+with+favo ring+drug+cartel-a01611776999 (Accessed August 25, 2010).

2. Ibid.

3. Ibid.

4. "Mexican police chief resigns amid threats," Associated Press, February 20, 2009, http://www.msnbc.msn.com/id/29303886 (Accessed August 23, 2009).

5. "Mexican police, soldiers killed in multicity attacks by drug gang," CNN, July 12, 2009, http://www.cnn.com/2009/WORLD/americas/07/11/mexico.attack/index.html (Accessed August 23, 2009).

6. *United States Road Atlas* (Ashland, Ohio: Bendon Publishing, 2009), 2–3.

7. Olga Rodriguez, "Report: Border Patrol confirms 29 incursions by Mexican officials into U.S. in 2006," *San Diego Union-Tribune*, January 9, 2008.

8. "Bernd Debusmann: In Mexico's drug wars, bullets and ballads," Reuters, July 9, 2008, http://www.reuters.com/article/idUSL0922436820080712 (Accessed August 23, 2009).

9. Mexico Security Memo, *Stratfor Global Intelligence*, July 28, 2008; National Drug Intelligence Center, "Marijuana," http://www.justice.gov/ndic/pubs11/18862/marijuan.htm (Accessed August 23, 2009).

10. Ken Ellingwood, "Toll mounts in Mexico's drug war," *Los Angeles Times*, June 3, 2008.

11. DEA, "OPERATION TAR PIT," http://www.justice.gov/dea/major/tarpit.htm (Accessed August 23, 2009).

12. Ibid.; Rod Ohira, "Feds charge 28 Hawaii suspects in far-reaching heroin operation," *Honolulu Star-Bulletin*, June 16, 2000.

13. Department of Justice Press Release (June 15, 2000), http://www.justice.gov/opa/pr/2000/June/342ag.htm (Accessed August 23, 2009).

14. Karima Haynes, "L.A. trafficker pleads guilty to heroin charges," *Los Angeles Times*, August 15, 2001.

15. Michael Newton, *The Encyclopedia of Serial Killers* (New York: Facts On File, 2000), 39–42.

16. Colleen Cook, *Mexico's Drug Cartels* (Washington, D.C.: Congressional Research Service, 2007), 1.

17. Ibid.

18. Howard LaFranchi, "A look inside a giant drug cartel," *Christian Science Monitor,* December 6, 1999.

19. Cook, 1.

20. "The World's Billionaires: #701 Joaquin Guzman Loera," *Forbes* (March 9, 2009), http://www.forbes.com/lists/2009/10/billionaires-2009-richest-people_Joaquin-Guzman-Loera_FS0Y.html (Accessed August 23, 2009).

21. Cook, 1.

22. Department of Justice press release (September 17, 2008), http://www.justice.gov/opa/pr/2008/September/08-ag-824.html (Accessed August 23, 2009).

23. "Mexico's 24 most wanted traffickers," *Los Angeles Times,* March 23, 2009.

24. "Grenade attack in Mexico breaks from deadly script," *New York Times,* September 24, 2008.

25. "Mexico's drug war: Cartel kills 12 federal officers," *Christian Science Monitor,* July 15, 2009.

26. Cook, 9.

27. Ibid., 10.

28. Kristin Bricker, "Over 10,000 dead: Is Mexican drug war violence ebbing?" The Narcosphere, http://narcosphere.narconews.com/notebook/kristin-bricker/2009/04/over-10000-dead-mexican-drug-war-violence-ebbing (Accessed August 23, 2009).

29. Cook, 11.

30. John Burnett, "Nuevo Laredo returns to normal as violence slows," NPR, http://www.npr.org/templates/story/story.php?storyId=99742620 (Accessed August 23, 2009).

31. Wesley Oliver, "17 dead in Acapulco shootout," Newser, http://www.newser.com/story/61233/17-dead-in-acapulco-shootout.html (Accessed August 23, 2009).

32. Cook, 12.

33. "10 Mexican police officers held in killings of 12 federal agents," CNN, July 19, 2009, http://www.cnn.com/2009/WORLD/americas/07/18/mexico.police.arrested (Accessed August 23, 2009).

34. Andrew Malone, "Thousands of Mexican soldiers pour into the country's most violent city in crackdown on drug gangs," *Daily Mail* (London), March 4, 2009.

35. Todd Bensman, "Most guns from raid traced to Texas," *San Antonio Express News,* March 31, 2009.

36. DEA, "DEA-Led Operation Puma Cages Southwest Border Drug Ring," http://www.justice.gov/dea/pubs/states/newsrel/dallas081607.html (Accessed August 23, 2009).

37. Ibid.

38. Nicole Spencer and Brian Wanko, "Merida Initiative Update: Mexico's Fight Against Organized Crime," Americas Society—Council of the Americas http://www.as-coa.org/article.php?id=1142 (Accessed August 23, 2009).

39. DEA, "DEA-Led Operation Puma Cages Southwest Border Drug Ring."

40. Department of Justice Press Release (March 3, 2009), http://www.justice.gov/usao/txn/PressRel09/cantu_jackson_maldonado_convict_pr.html (Accessed August 23, 2009).

41. Darren Meritz, "Lawmakers to evaluate Merida Initiative's success," *El Paso Times,* February 8, 2009.

42. U.S. Department of State, "Plan Colombia," http://merln.ndu.edu/archivepdf/colombia/State/1042.pdf (Accessed August 23, 2009); Center for International Police press release (April 15, 2006), http://ciponline.

org/colombia/060415coca.pdf (Accessed August 23, 2009).

43. Katherine Peters, "DEA: Mexican drug violence is a sign of progress, not failure," GovernmentExecutive. com, http://www.govexec.com/dailyfed/0409/041509kp1.htm (Accessed August 23, 2009).

Chapter 4

1. DEA, "DEA, Coast Guard Make Record Maritime Cocaine Seizure," http://www.justice.gov/dea/pubs/states/newsrel/wdo032107.html (Accessed August 25, 2009).
2. Ibid.
3. Ibid.
4. "Nicknames and Street Names for Cocaine," The Canyon, http://www.thecyn.com/cocaine-rehab/cocaine-street-names.html (Accessed August 25, 2009).
5. "A Brief History of Cocaine," MyAddiction.com, http://www.myaddiction.com/categories/cocaine_timeline.html (Accessed August 25, 2009).
6. Ibid.
7. Ibid.
8. Ibid.
9. Ibid.
10. Pub.L. 91-513, 84 Stat. 1236, enacted October 27, 1970, codified at 21 U.S.C. § 801 et. seq.
11. "A Brief History of Cocaine."
12. "Roberto Suárez Gómez," Encyclopedia Britannica, http://www.britannica.com/EBchecked/topic/713761/Roberto-Suarez-Gomez (Accessed August 25, 2009).
13. Felia Allum and Renate Siebert, *Organized Crime and the Challenge to Democracy* (London: Routledge, 2003), 98–100.
14. Kevin Riley, *Snow Job?: The War Against International Cocaine Traf-* *ficking* (Edison, N.J.: Transaction, 1996), 170, 178, 181.

15. U.S. Immigration and Customs Enforcement, "History of the ICE Investigation into Colombia's Cali Drug Cartel and the Rodriguez-Orejuela Brothers," http://www.ice.gov/pi/news/factsheets/califs031105.htm (Accessed August 25, 2009).
16. Ron Chepesiuk, "The Fall of the Cali Cartel," *Crime Magazine,* October 21, 2006, http://www.crime-magazine.com/fall-cali-cartel-0 (Accessed August 25, 2009).
17. Kevin Noblet, "Drug lords start 'war' in Colombia," *Philadelphia Inquirer,* August 25, 1989.
18. "Pablo Escobar Biography," Biography.com, http://www.biography.com/articles/Pablo-Escobar-9542497 (Accessed August 25, 2009).
19. "U.S. and Swiss Authorities Sign Agreement to Split More Than $175 million in Illegal Drug Proceeds," Department of Justice Press Release (December 18, 1998), http://www.justice.gov/opa/pr/1998/December/599ag.htm (Accessed August 25, 2009).
20. "Pablo Escobar Biography."
21. Ibid.
22. DEA, "United States Announces RICO Charges Against Leadership of Colombia's Most Powerful Cocaine Cartel," http://www.justice.gov/dea/pubs/pressrel/pr050604.html (Accessed August 25, 2009).
23. Chris Kraul, "Colombian drug lord shot dead," *Los Angeles Times,* February 2, 2008.
24. DEA, "Stats & Facts," http://www.justice.gov/dea/statistics.html#seizures (Accessed August 25, 2009).

25. "Fast Drug Facts: Cocaine and Cocaine Arrests," 12 Steps Again, http://12stepsagain. com/2009/05/04/fast-drug-facts-cocaine-and-cocaine-arrests (Accessed August 25, 2009).

26. Office of National Drug Control Policy, *The Price and Purity of Illicit Drugs: 1981 Through the Second Quarter of 2003* (Washington, D.C.: Executive Office of the President, 2004), 58–59.

27. *National Household Survey on Drug Abuse: Population Estimates 1998* (Washington, D.C.: U.S. Department of Health and Human Services, 1999), 37–39.

28. National Drug Intelligence Center, "Crack Cocaine Fast Facts," http://www.justice.gov/ndic/pubs3/3978/index.htm (Accessed August 25, 2009).

29. Department of Justice, "The CIA-Contra-Crack Cocaine Controversy," http://www. justice.gov/oig/special/9712/ch01p1.htm (Accessed August 25, 2009).

30. Federal Bureau of Investigation, "Crips and Bloods Drug Gang," http://foia.fbi.gov/foiaindex/crips-bloods.htm (Accessed August 25, 2009).

31. PBS, *Crips and Bloods: Made in America,* http://www.pbs.org/independentlens/cripsandbloods (Accessed August 25, 2009).

32. Grace Livingstone, *Inside Colombia: Drugs, Democracy, and War* (Piscataway, N.J.: Rutgers University Press, 2004), 55.

33. "Prestigious but failing Colombian paper ceases daily editions," *Miami Herald,* August 30, 2001.

34. "Drug cartel tied to crash of Colombia jet," *Chicago Sun-Times,* November 28, 1989.

35. "Colombia truck bomb kills 35, many injured in blast," *Miami Herald,* December 7, 1989.

36. Tom Wells, "25 dead, 163 injured as car bombs explode in two Colombian cities," *Philadelphia Inquirer,* May 13, 1990.

37. "Intent of Colombia bombing unclear," *Dallas Morning News,* February 19, 1991.

38. ABC Evening News, April 15, 1993, http://tvnews.vanderbilt.edu/program.pl?ID= 147115 (Accessed August 25, 2009).

39. "Medellin Cartel," Reference.com, http://www.reference.com/browse/medellin+cartel (Accessed August 25, 2009).

40. CIA, *The World Factbook,* "Illicit Drugs," https://www.cia.gov/library/publications/the-world-factbook/fields/2086.html (Accessed August 25, 2009).

41. DEA, "DEA Dismantles Large International Drug and Money Laundering Organization," http://www.justice.gov/dea/pubs/pressrel/pr120805.html (Accessed August 25, 2009).

42. DEA, "Major Operations," http://www.justice.gov/dea/major/major.htm (Accessed August 25, 2009).

43. DEA, "DEA Dismantles Large International Drug and Money Laundering Organization."

44. Ibid.

45. DEA, "Cocaine," http://www.justice.gov/dea/concern/cocaine.html (Accessed August 25, 2009).

46. Ibid.

Chapter 5

1. DEA, "Heroin Traffickers Used Puppies to Smuggle Drugs," http://www.justice.gov/dea/pubs/pressrel/

pr020106.html (Accessed August 25, 2009).

2. Ibid.

3. Ibid.

4. National Institute on Drug Abuse, "NIDA InfoFacts: Heroin," http://www.nida.nih.gov/infofacts/heroin.html (Accessed August 25, 2009).

5. "History of Heroin and Opium Timeline," Heroin Addiction, http://www.heroinaddiction.com/heroin_timeline.html (Accessed August 25, 2009).

6. Ibid.

7. Ibid.

8. Ibid.

9. Edward Brecher, "The Consumers Union Report—Licit and Illicit Drugs," Schaffer Library of Drug Policy, http://druglibrary.org/schaffer/Library/studies/cu/cumenu.htm (Accessed August 25, 2009).

10. Ibid.

11. "History of Heroin and Opium Timeline."

12. Brecher.

13. "History of Heroin and Opium Timeline."

14. Ibid.

15. Ibid.

16. Ibid.

17. "Khun Sa," *The Times* (London), November 5, 2007.

18. Ibid.

19. Clarence Lusane, *Pipe Dream Blues: Racism and the War on Drugs* (Boston: South End Press, 1999), 219.

20. Julia Preston, "Decline seen in numbers of people here illegally," *New York Times,* July 31, 2008.

21. CIA, *The World Factbook*, "Illicit Drugs," https://www.cia.gov/library/publications/the-world-factbook/fields/2086.html (Accessed August 25, 2009).

22. Joseph Treaster, "Colombia's drug lords add new product: heroin for

U.S.," *New York Times,* January 14, 1992.

23. "History of Heroin and Opium Timeline."

24. "United Nations Press Conference on Afghanistan Opium Survey 2004," United Nations, http://www.un.org/News/briefings/docs/2004/McCleanBriefing_041118.doc.htm (Accessed August 25, 2009).

25. United Nations International Drug Control Programme, *Afghanistan: Annual Opium Poppy Survey 2001,* http://www.unodc.org/pdf/publications/report_2001-10-16_1.pdf (Accessed August 25, 2009).

26. Graeme Smith, "Portrait of the enemy," *Globe and Mail* (Toronto), March 22, 2008.

27. United Nations Office on Drugs and Crime, "Opium Amounts to Half of Afghanistan's GDP in 2007, Reports UNODC," http://www.unodc.org/unodc/en/press/ releases/opium-amounts-to-half-of-afghanistans-gdp-in-2007,-reports-unodc.html (Accessed August 25, 2009).

28. CIA, *The World Factbook*, "Illicit Drugs," https://www.cia.gov/library/publications/the-world-factbook/fields/2086.html (Accessed August 25, 2009).

29. Interpol, "Heroin," http://www.interpol.com/Public/Drugs/heroin/default.asp (Accessed August 25, 2009).

30. Mike La Sorte, "Gaetano Badalamenti and the Pizza Connection," AmericanMafia.com, http://www.americanmafia.com/Feature_Articles_271.html (Accessed August 25, 2009).

31. Ibid.

32. Ibid.

33. Ibid.

34. Ibid.

35. Ibid.; *The World Factbook*.

36. *The World Factbook*; Interpol.
37. *The World Factbook*; Interpol.
38. PBS, "From Poppy to Heroin," http://www.pbs.org/wnet/wide angle/episodes/bitter-harvest/from-poppy-to-heroin/from-poppy-to-heroin-introduction/3167 (Accessed August 25, 2009).
39. United Nations Office on Drugs and Crime, *World Drug Report 2006 Volume 2: Statistics* (Vienna, Austria: UNODC, 2006), 365–366.
40. Office of National Drug Control Policy, *The Price and Purity of Illicit Drugs: 1981 Through the Second Quarter of 2003* (Washington, D.C.: Executive Office of the President, 2004), 62–63.
41. *The World Factbook*.
42. DEA, "Stats & Facts," http://www.justice.gov/dea/statistics.html#seizures (Accessed August 25, 2009).
43. DEA, "Major Operations," http://www.justice.gov/dea/major/major.htm (Accessed August 25, 2009).
44. Schaffer Library of Drug Policy, "Estimated Per Capita Death Rates by Drugs," http://www.druglibrary.org/think/~jnr/drugmort.htm (Accessed August 25, 2009).
45. Virginia Department of Health, "Cocaine, Heroin, Morphine and MDMA Deaths, 2004-2006," http://www.vdh.state.va.us/medExam/documents/2009/pdfs/IllegalDrugs.pdf (Accessed August 25, 2009).
46. Scott Bernard Nelson, "Heroin deaths on the rise, 2007 statistics show," *The Oregonian* (Portland), May 13, 2008.
47. Nassau County, N.Y., "Heroin Prevention," http://www.nassaucountyny.gov/heroinprevention.html (Accessed August 25, 2010).
48. Andrew Byrne, *Addict in the Family: How to Cope with the Long Haul* (Redfern: New South Wales, Australia, 1996), 33–34.
49. Stanton Peele, "The Persistent, Dangerous Myth of Heroin Overdose," The Stanton Peele Addiction Web site, http://www.peele.net/lib/heroinoverdose.html (Accessed August 25, 2009).

Chapter 6
1. DEA, "Middle School Principal Arrested for Selling Meth," http://www.justice.gov/dea/pubs/states/newsrel/phila022807.html (Accessed August 28, 2009).
2. Ibid.
3. Office of National Drug Control Policy, "The National Methamphetamine Drug Conference," http://www.ncjrs.gov/ondcppubs/publications/drugfact/methconf/plenary4.html (Accessed August 28, 2009).
4. Outlaws World, http://www.outlawsmcworld.com (Accessed August 28, 2009).
5. Wes Laurie, "Outlaw Motorcycle Clubs: The Best of the Worst," Associated Content, http://www.associatedcontent.com/article/350308/outlaw_motorcycle_clubs_the_best_of_pg4.html?cat=27 (Accessed August 5, 2010).
6. Hells Angels Motorcycle Club World, http://www.hells-angels.com/?HA=charters (Accessed August 28, 2009).
7. Michael Buck, "Ex-principal John Acerra released from prison," *Express-Times* (Bethlehem, Pa.), June 3, 2009.
8. DEA, "Methamphetamine," http://www.justice.gov/dea/concern/meth.html (Accessed August 28, 2009).
9. "RCMP paid Hells Angels informant," *Vancouver Sun*, September 13, 2006.

10. Maryland Gangs, "Pagans," http://gangs.umd.edu/wfrmGangsinmdDetail.aspx?id=Pagans (Accessed August 5, 2010).

11. Bandidos Motorcycle Club World-wide, http://www.bandidosmc.dk/chapters.asp (Accessed August 28, 2009).

12. Stephen Kinzer, "Biker wars in the land of 'the Little Mermaid,'" *New York Times,* May 6, 1996.

13. IdahoGangs.com, "Bandidos," http://idahogangs.com/index.php?option=com_content&task=blogcategory&id=140&Itemid=325 (Accessed August 5, 2010).

14. The Vaults of Erowid, "Metham-phetamine Timeline," http://www.erowid.org/chemicals/meth/meth_timeline.php (Accessed August 28, 2009).

15. Ibid.

16. DEA, "Methamphetamine," http://www.justice.gov/dea/concern/meth.html (Accessed August 28, 2009).

17. DEA, "Operation Pill Crusher Nets 10 Arrests," http://www.justice.gov/dea/pubs/states/newsrel/nyc060107.html (Accessed August 28, 2009).

18. DEA, "Stats & Facts," http://www.justice.gov/dea/statistics.html#seizures (Accessed August 28, 2009).

19. DEA, "Maps of Methamphetamine Lab Incidents," http://www.justice.gov/dea/concern/map_lab_seizures.html (Accessed August 28, 2009).

20. DEA, "OPERATION META," http://www.justice.gov/dea/major/meta.htm (Accessed August 28, 2009); DEA, "DEA Confirms Arrest by Mexican Authorities of AMEZCUA-CONTRERAS Brothers," http://www.justice.gov/dea/pubs/pressrel/pr980602.htm (Accessed August 28, 2009).

21. DEA, "Operation Mountain Express," http://www.justice.gov/dea/major/mountainexpress.htm (Accessed August 28, 2009).

22. DEA, "Operation Triple X," http://www.justice.gov/dea/major/triplex.html (Accessed August 28, 2009).

23. DEA, "More than 100 Arrested in Nationwide Methamphetamine Investigation," http://www.justice.gov/dea/major/me3.html (Accessed August 28, 2009).

24. DEA, "DEA Takedown Nets Multi-Ton Pseudoephedrine Seizure," http://www.justice.gov/dea/pubs/pressrel/pr011802.html (Accessed August 28, 2009).

25. DEA, "Operation Northern Star," http://www.justice.gov/dea/major/northern_star/index.html (Accessed August 28, 2009).

26. DEA, "Yuma-based Methamph-etamine Trafficking Organization Dismantled," http://www.justice.gov/dea/pubs/states/newsrel/phnx120904.html (Accessed August 28, 2009).

27. DEA, "Operation Global Warming," http://www.justice.gov/dea/pubs/states/newsrel/seattle031305.html (Accessed August 28, 2009).

28. DEA, "DEA Fractures Major Meth Pipeline Into U.S.," http://www.justice.gov/dea/pubs/pressrel/pr081905.html (Accessed August 28, 2009).

29. DEA, "Attorney General Gonzales and DEA Administrator Tandy Announce Results of Unprec-edented National Anti-Meth Initiative," http://www.justice.gov/dea/pubs/pressrel/pr083005.html (Accessed August 28, 2009).

30. DEA, "U.K. Couple Face Extradi-tion for Supplying Chemicals to

U.S. Meth Labs," http://www.justice
.gov/dea/pubs/states/newsrel/phnx
013007.html (Accessed August 28,
2009).

31. DEA, "Operation GhostRider
    Nets 28 Arrests, Gang Targeted,"
    http://www.justice.gov/dea/pubs/
    states/newsrel/denver051407.html
    (Accessed August 29, 2009).

32. DEA, "Mexican-Based Interna-
    tional Drug Trafficking Organiza-
    tion Takes Big Hit in US," http://
    www.justice.gov/dea/pubs/states/
    newsrel/atlanta121107.html
    (Accessed August 29, 2009).

33. DEA, "Operation Pill Crusher Nets
    10 Arrests," http://www.justice.gov/
    dea/pubs/states/newsrel/nyc060107.
    html (Accessed August 28, 2009).

34. Ibid.

35. Ibid.

36. DEA, "DEA Nets Largest Meth
    Seizure Ever in New Jersey," http://
    www.justice.gov/dea/pubs/states/
    newsrel/2008/nwk120208.html
    (Accessed August 29, 2009).

37. DEA, "New Data Show Significant
    Disruptions in U.S. Methamphet-
    amine, Cocaine Markets; Price
    of Meth Soars 73 Percent; Purity
    Down by Nearly A Third," http://
    www.justice.gov/dea/pubs/pressrel/
    pr110807.html (Accessed August
    29, 2009).

38. DEA, "Stats & Facts," http://www.
    justice.gov/dea/statistics.html#sei
    zures (Accessed August 29, 2009).

39. DEA, "Maps of Methamphetamine
    Lab Incidents," http://www.justice.
    gov/dea/concern/map_lab_seizures.
    html (Accessed August 29, 2009).

Chapter 7

1. DEA, "Large Scale Cocaine Trafficker Sentenced to Life in Prison
   for Drug Trafficking and Money
   Laundering," http://www.justice.
   gov/dea/pubs/states/newsrel/2009/
   phnx121109b.html (Accessed
   August 27, 2009).

2. Ibid.

3. International Money Laundering
   Information Network, https://
   www.imolin.org/amlid2/browse_
   countries.jsp (Accessed August 27,
   2009).

4. U.S. Department of the Treasury,
   *Bank Secrecy Act/Anti-Money
   Laundering Comptroller's Hand-
   book,* http://www.occ.treas.gov/
   handbook/bsa.pdf (Accessed
   August 27, 2009).

5. Julia Layton, "How money laundering works," How Stuff Works,
   http://money.howstuffworks.com/
   money-laundering.htm (Accessed
   August 27, 2009).

6. John Kerry and Hank Brown, *The
   BCCI Affair: A Report to the Com-
   mittee on Foreign Relations, United
   States Senate,* FAS, http://www.fas.
   org/irp/congress/1992_rpt/bcci
   (Accessed August 27, 2009).

7. Ibid.

8. Ibid.

9. Ibid.

10. Ibid.

11. Financial Action Task Force
    (FATF), http://www.fatf-gafi.org/
    pages/0,2978, en_32250379_32235
    720_1_1_1_1,00.html (Accessed
    August 27, 2009).

12. Caribbean Financial Action Task
    Force (CATF), http://www.cfatf-
    gafic.org (Accessed August 27,
    2009).

13. The Asia/Pacific Group on Money
    Laundering (APG), http://www.
    apgml.org (Accessed August 27,
    2009).

14. Council of Europe, "MONEYVAL,"
    http://www.coe.int/t/dghl/monitor
    ing/moneyval (Accessed August
    27, 2009).

15. GAFISUD, http://www.imolin. org/imolin/GAFISUDintro.html (Accessed August 27, 2009).

16. MENAFATF, http://www.menafatf. org (Accessed August 27, 2009).

17. EAG, http://www.eurasiangroup. org (Accessed August 27, 2009).

18. DEA, "Foreign Field Divisions," http://www.justice.gov/dea/ pubs/international/foreign.html (Accessed August 27, 2009).

19. United Nations General Assembly Special Session on the World Drug Problem, "Money Laundering," http://www.un.org/ga/20special/ featur/launder.htm (Accessed August 27, 2009); Ron Chepesiuk, *The Bullet or the Bribe: Taking Down Colombia's Cali Drug Cartel* (Santa Barbara, Calif.: Praeger, 2003), 103–105.

20. DEA, "OPERATION DINERO," http://www.justice.gov/dea/major/ dinero.htm (Accessed August 27, 2009).

21. DEA, "OPERATION JUNO," http:// www.justice.gov/dea/major/juno. htm (Accessed August 27, 2009).

22. DEA, "Statement From DEA Administrator Karen P. Tandy on Operation Double Trouble," http:// www.justice.gov/dea/pubs/pressrel/ pr082903.html (Accessed August 27, 2009).

23. DEA, "United States Requests Extradition of Cali Cartel Leaders From Colombia on Money Laundering Charges," http://www. justice.gov/dea/pubs/states/newsrel/ nyc030404.html (Accessed August 27, 2009); "Colombian drug lords jailed in US," BBC News, September 27, 2006.

24. DEA, "Operation Money Clip Dismantles Major Money Laundering and Drug Operation," http://www.ju

stice.gov/dea/pubs/pressrel/pr1019 04.html (Accessed August 27, 2009).

25. Anslee Willett, "Drug pipeline ran through Peyton ranch," *The Gazette* (Colorado Springs, Colo.), October 20, 2004.

26. DEA, "DEA's 'Money Trail Initiative' Cuts Flow of Cash to Cartels," http://www.justice.gov/dea/pubs/ pressrel/pr071905.html (Accessed August 27, 2009).

27. DEA, "Major Cocaine, Meth and Money Laundering Organization Dismantled," http://www.justice. gov/dea/pubs/pressrel/pr101305a. html (Accessed August 27, 2009).

28. DEA, "DEA Aids in the Arrest of International Money Manager Accused of Laundering $1 Billion in Illegal Proceeds," http://www. justice.gov/dea/pubs/pressrel/ pr012306.html (Accessed August 27, 2009); United States Department of Justice, U.S. Attorney, Southern District of New York, press release (March 14, 2007), http://www.justice.gov/tax/usao- press/2007/txdv07tremblaysen tencingpr.pdf (Accessed August 27, 2009).

29. DEA, "56 charged in drug trafficking & money laundering indictments," http://www.justice. gov/dea/pubs/states/newsrel/ carib100606.html (Accessed August 27, 2009).

30. DEA, "Statement by Administrator Karen P. Tandy on Two Hundred and Seven Million in Drug Money Seized in Mexico City," http:// www.justice.gov/dea/pubs/pressrel/ pr032007.html (Accessed August 27, 2009).

31. DEA, "U.S. Seizes Over $5.6 Million From Dubai-Based Money Launderer," http://www.justice.

gov/dea/pubs/states/newsrel/
nyc050407.html (Accessed August
27, 2009).

32. DEA, "Over Par and Under Arrest:
Golf Co. Execs Busted," http://www.
justice.gov/dea/pubs/states/newsrel/
sd022708.html (Accessed August
27, 2009).

33. DEA, "U.S. Announces Indictment of Heads of Colombia's
D.M.G. Group for Money Laundering," http://www.justice.gov/
dea/pubs/states/newsrel/2009/
nyc031909.html (Accessed
August 27, 2009).

34. DEA, "Colombian Drug and
Money Laundering Ring Shattered,"
http://www.justice.gov/dea/pubs/
pressrel/pr061405.html (Accessed
August 27, 2009).

35. Ibid.

36. Ibid.

37. Ibid.

38. Howrey LLP, "Black Market Peso Exchange at issue in
Kuehne money-laundering
case," http://www.howrey.com/
black-market-peso-exchange-at-
issue-in-kuehne-money-launder-
ing-case-03-09-2009 (Accessed
August 27, 2009).

39. DEA, "Money Laundering Threat
Assessment Released," http://www.
justice.gov/dea/pubs/pressrel/
pr011106.html (Accessed August
27, 2009).

40. Ibid.

Chapter 8.

1. DEA, "DEA Museum & Visitors
Center," http://www.deamuseum.
org/museum_aboutus.html
(Accessed August 27, 2009).

2. Ibid.

3. DEA, "Spencer Stafford," http://
www.justice.gov/dea/agency/10bios.

htm#stafford (Accessed August 5,
2010).

4. DEA, "Wall of Honor," http://www.
justice.gov/dea/agency/10_list.htm
(Accessed August 27, 2009)

5. DEA, "Wall of Honor."

6. Ibid.

7. Ibid.

8. Ibid.

9. Ibid.

10. Ibid.

11. Ibid.

12. Ibid.

13. Ibid.

14. Ibid.

15. Ibid.

16. DEA, "Aviation Division," http://
www.justice.gov/dea/programs/
aviation.htm (Accessed August 27,
2009).

17. DEA, "Wall of Honor," http://www.
justice.gov/dea/agency/10_list.htm
(Accessed August 27, 2009).

18. Ibid.

19. Ibid.

20. Ibid.

21. Ibid.

22. Ibid.

23. Ibid.

24. DEA, "1970–1975," http://www.
justice.gov/dea/pubs/history/1970
-1975.html (Accessed August 27,
2009).

25. DEA, "Wall of Honor," http://www.
justice.gov/dea/agency/10_list.htm
(Accessed August 27, 2009).

26. Ibid.

27. Ibid.

28. Ibid.

29. Ibid.

30. Ibid.

31. Ibid.

32. DEA, "1985–1990," http://www.
justice.gov/dea/pubs/history/1985
-1990.html (Accessed August 27,
2009).

33. "Mexico officials said to thwart murder probe," *Washington Post*, December 4, 1992.

34. *Alvarez-Machain v. United States*, 331 F.3d 604, 610 (9th Cir. 2003).

35. DEA, "Guilty Verdict Relating to Murder of Two DEA Agents,"

http://www.justice.gov/dea/pubs/pressrel/pr092805.html (Accessed August 27, 2009).

36. DEA, "Wall of Honor," http://www.justice.gov/dea/agency/10_list.htm (Accessed August 27, 2009).

37. Ibid.

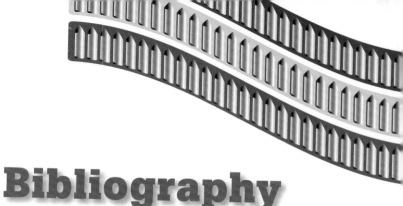

Bibliography

Baum, Dan. *Smoke and Mirrors: The War on Drugs and the Politics of Failure.* New York: Back Bay Books, 1997.

Bertram, Eva, Morris Blachman, Kenneth Sharpe, and Peter Andreas. *Drug War Politics: The Price of Denial.* Berkeley: University of California Press, 1996.

Chepesiuk, Ron. *Drug Lords: The Rise and Fall of the Cali Cartel.* Preston, U.K.:Milo Books, 2005.

Clifford, Tom. *Inside The DEA.* Bloomington, Ind.: AuthorHouse, 2005.

Doyle, Paul. *Hot Shots and Heavy Hits: Tales of an Undercover Drug Agent.* Boston: Northeastern University Press, 2005.

Drug Enforcement Administration. *A Tradition of Excellence: The History of the DEA from 1973 to 1998.* Washington, D.C.: DEA, 1999.

Eddy, Paul, Hugo Sabogal, and Sara Walden. *The Cocaine Wars.* New York: W.W. Norton, 1988.

Hartstein, Max. *The War on Drugs: The Worst Addiction of All.* Bloomington, Ind.: AuthorHouse, 2003.

Mares, David. *Drug Wars and Coffeehouses: The Political Economy of the International Drug Trade.* Washington, D.C.: CQ Press, 2005.

McCoy, Alfred. *The Politics of Heroin: CIA Complicity in the Global Drug Trade.* Chicago: Lawrence Hill, 2003.

Messick, Hank. *Of Grass and Snow: The Secret Criminal Elite.* Englewood Cliffs, N.J.: Prentice Hall, 1979.

Robbins, David. *Heavy Traffic: 30 Years of Headlines and Major Ops From the Case Files of the DEA.* New York: Chamberlain Brothers, 2005.

Scott, Peter. *Drugs, Oil, and War: The United States in Afghanistan, Colombia, and Indochina.* Lanham, Md.: Rowman & Littlefield, 2003.

Scott, Peter, and Jonathan Marshall. *Cocaine Politics: Drugs, Armies, and the CIA in Central America.* Berkeley: University of California Press, 1998.

Valentine, Douglas. *The Strength of the Wolf: The Secret History of America's War on Drugs.* London: Verso, 2006.

Further Resources

Print

Bowden, Mark. *Killing Pablo: The Hunt for the World's Greatest Outlaw*. New York: Penguin, 2002. Case history of Colombia's most notorious drug lord.

Fleming, Doug. *Drug Wars: Narco Warfare in the 21st Century*. Charleston, S.C.: BookSurge, 2008. Assesses the war on drugs in a new century.

Gugliotta, Guy, and Jeff Leen. *Kings of Cocaine: Inside the Medellin Cartel*. New York: Simon & Schuster, 1989. History of Colombia's most violent drug cartel.

Miron, Jeffrey. *Drug War Crimes: The Consequences of Prohibition*. New Brunswick, N.J.: Independent Institute, 2004. Critical view of the war on drugs and its impact on society.

Speziale, Jerry. *Without a Badge: Undercover in the World's Deadliest Criminal Organization*. New York: Kensington, 2003. Memoir of an undercover narcotics officer.

Online

Bureau of Justice Statistics
http://bjs.ojp.usdoj.gov/
Analyzes criminal trends in America, including drug-related crimes.

Drug Enforcement Administration
http://www.justice.gov/dea/index.htm
Official DEA Web site.

Drug War Clock
http://www.drugsense.org/wodclock.htm
A running scorecard of statistics related to the war on drugs.

Drug War Facts
http://www.drugwarfacts.org/cms
A critical assessment of the federal war on drugs.

Index

About the Author

Michael Newton has published 235 books since 1977, with 15 forthcoming from various houses through 2011. His history of the Florida Ku Klux Klan (*The Invisible Empire*, 2001) won the Florida Historical Society's 2002 Rembert Patrick Award for "Best Book in Florida History," and his *Encyclopedia of Cryptozoology* was one of the American Library Association's Outstanding Reference Works in 2006. His nonfiction work includes numerous volumes for Chelsea House Publishers and Facts On File.